CHRISTIAN POLITICAL CORRECTNESS

How False Doctrine Helps
Shape Christian Nationalism

Philip Joel Walls

Copyright © 2024 Philip Joel Walls

All rights reserved.

No part of this book may be reproduced, stored in a retrieval system, or transmitted by any means, electronic, mechanical, photocopying, recording, or otherwise, without written permission from the author.

ISBN (Paperback): 979-8-9905012-0-1
ISBN (eBook): 979-8-9904362-9-9

Contents

Introduction v

Chapter 1: Christian Nationalism –
War in the Name of Christ 1

Chapter 2: Persecution and Fighting Back 33

Chapter 3: Paying Taxes to Caesar 73

Chapter 4: The Founding Fathers 89

Chapter 5: A True Christian Nation 113

Endnotes 139

"Patriotism is the last refuge of a scoundrel."

~ Samuel Johnson, April 7, 1775 ~

Introduction

Many faithful believers will claim the evidence presented in this book is antagonistic toward Christian traditions in the United States of America. Though my reply is apologetic, they would be right. Let it be known to my family, friends, readers, and anyone else who stumbles across these pages...

> Speaking heresy against false doctrine is
> not an offense to Christ.

If you search the Christian New Testament, you will find there is not one single book that fails to forcefully condemn false doctrine. Speaking truth was paramount to the apostles, and it should be as equally predominant in our lives.

For those who may initially be offended by the biblical and historical evidence presented, they should, with all due respect, prepare in advance to be offended and continue reading. The truth hurts, as they say. But this hurt is a necessary pain if we are to allow the healing process to begin.

It is passed time we open our eyes to the gospel message missing from Politically Correct Christianity. We will have become empty vessels if we seek to appease the traditions of this fallen world while ignoring the spiritual fornication taking place among the body of believers.

At certain times throughout history, books of this nature could land a person in tight quarters. Those who dared to distribute anti-establishment literature would be silenced by the guillotines or burned at the stake, or worse. By proclaiming their faith according to the teachings of Christ as opposed to blindly following religious fanatics (or a state-sponsored religion), many were, and are, sentenced to death.

Luckily for Americans, we live in a land that is, for now, still a country where "freedom of religion" is somewhat permitted. Even if it were not, even if we were placing our lives on the line according to our faith, we must never cower in fear to the wicked who seek to silence the teachings of Christ. Persecution has been a reality for God's people all throughout history. This fate is possible for anyone speaking truth in a world encompassed by Satanic lies. We must always keep in mind how eternal life awaits the peaceful martyrs. In the event of a loved one's death at the hand of persecution or tyranny, we can rest assured that God has carried them gracefully through to the other side. They are very well taken care of. We who are left behind must continue to refuse to bow down to any doctrine that seeks to diminish the truth of God and His only begotten son while giving rise to personal interest, worldly endeavors, comfortable religion, or Christian political correctness. All of which are continuously leading souls as gullible sheep to the slaughter.

The day is coming when Christ will return to fulfill all things. As promised, we will finally be free from the immaculate deceptions attacking us on all fronts. Until that day, we must continue speaking out against the Christian heretics of our age who appear steadfast in twisting scripture, creating false doctrine, instituting divisions in the body of believers, and worshiping the idols of politically correct religion.

Those who claim to be equal with the apostles often quote *the Holy Bible* in an attempt to persuade their peers. With all meekness and sincerity, we too must quote the words of Jesus to bring everything into context. We must offer a fullness of the scriptures without diminishing ourselves to inter-denominational soundbites.

Do not be afraid of the opposition we face in this current earth age. We must always stand fast in the truth.

> Therefore, put on God's complete armor, that you may be able to resist and stand your ground on the evil day [of danger], and having done all [the crisis demands], to stand [firmly in your place]. 14Stand therefore [hold your ground], having tightened the belt of truth around your loins and having put on the breastplate of integrity and of moral rectitude and right standing with God. (Ephesians 6:13-14; AMP)

~

Before we get started, we need to talk about the biblical definition of righteousness. The word "righteous" does not mean we are somehow holier than other people. Righteousness is to be *right* in the eyes of God. To be *truthful* in the eyes of God. To be *just* and *faithful* in the eyes of God. This is the definition of righteousness. To be righteous is to be truthful, and correct. It is to make the "right" decisions as a result of knowing God's will in our lives.

When Jesus spoke to his apostles, "Blessed are they which do hunger and thirst after *right*eousness: for they shall be filled", he was stating that those who seek to be in accordance with truth, in accordance with what is "right" in the eyes of God the Father, they will receive their righteousness by faith.

Abraham was credited with righteousness not because he was a perfect man, but because he believed the truth of what God had communicated to him. He was *right* when he made the choice to leave his home and venture out into the wilderness by faith alone that God would do what He said He would do. Abraham believed God's words were both true and the "right" thing to do. Believing in God's words, His power, His authority, and remaining firm in His truth is how we attain and sustain a level of *right*eousness in our lives.

Knowing now the true definition of righteousness, what happens if we allow "God and Country" to stand in place of Christ's testimony to the world? What happens when we allow the traditions of the established church, or the traditions of the established 'law of the land' to take precedence over the words of our King Jehoshua? What happens when we adhere to the temporal status quo without considering the eternal nature of what is *right* and *truthful* in the eyes of God?

The answer of course is that when we teach politically correct Christianity in place of *right*eousness and historical truth, we are opening the door to blasphemous idolatries.

We Christians claim the United States of America is and was founded as a Christian nation. We claim God is on **our** side. We print "in God we trust" on all our money. If it is true to suggest we trust in Jehovah alone, and this is **His** nation, and that we trust in His only begotten son Jehoshua for salvation, and that the USA was in fact a nation built on "the first precepts of Christianity" by the power of God the

Father…then we would be wise to remember God's promises given to *His* people.

In this book, we will be addressing several topics that tie into the fundamental principles of who American Christians claim to be as a nation and what led to the institution of the United States of America. Not least of which are 1) religious persecution under tyrannical rule, 2) money and unfair taxation, 3) what a true Christian nation would look like, and 4) an ever-growing movement called Christian Nationalism.

We will examine biblical and historical evidence to illustrate how the business of Government in the United States of America is not now, nor ever has been, and certainly was not founded upon Christian principles. It will be shown that the testimony of Jesus Christ proves the "American experiment" to be nothing more than an unintended heretical grift at best, and outright anti-Christ idolatry at its worst.

In thinking forward to what I am about to write, it would be appropriate to quote Pastor Gerry Burney from Target Truth Ministries[1] when he said the following.

> "I do not claim to be a prophet, but I do claim to read the bible and pay attention to what God states."

CHAPTER 1

CHRISTIAN NATIONALISM – WAR IN THE NAME OF CHRIST

For what is a man profited, if he shall gain the whole world, and lose his own soul? (Matthew 16:26)

A vast number of American Christians are growing increasingly comfortable with what can only be described as a dual-allegiance, theo-political system of government. Their desire is to live in a nation who's reigning King is Jesus Christ, while simultaneously crowning their chosen politicians as, well... someone else. As things become more and more unstable in the United States, most Christians are latching onto the idea of "Christian Nationalism". To some, this may be the only way to save America from the unprecedented corruption in our government.

Christian Nationalists do not believe it is enough for Christ to reign in our hearts or to deny this fallen world as Christ commanded. Rather, they believe Christ must also reign through us, his acting subjects, as a militant force to defend his Father's legal precedence in our beloved homeland.

Richard the Lionheart was often quoted as saying, "*This is God's country*" or "*God is with us!*" as he and his Christian soldiers charged into battle. We have a similar mentality today, and *we* will do all *His* goodwill and pleasure to keep our freedoms intact. We believe Jesus must govern the moral values of the subject population, while Christian Nationalist leaders govern (by any means necessary, including warfare) the legal affairs outlined in the Bible via God's universal judgement.

One of the more obvious reasons we believe such things is that we were educated from a very young age how *the United States of America was founded as a Christian nation*. And therefore, we must defend our "God" given constitutional republic against all enemies foreign, and domestic.

But does our militant attitude toward this fallen world live up to the gospel of Jesus Christ?

> Jesus said, "My kingdom is not of this world. If it were, my servants would fight to prevent my arrest by the Jewish leaders. But now my kingdom is from another place." (John 18:36; NIV)

One item Christian Nationalists fail to acknowledge is the monumental difference between the honest God-fearing Christians who settled peacefully with America's native inhabitants and those who would later provoke a war for independence from the British crown. It was this small group of well-organized and well-motivated individuals who founded this new republic providing a means to an end for their own interests, and not the interests of Christ or our heavenly Father.

This, dear reader, is an easily proven fact of history as will be noted continuously throughout this book. Ironically, it was this newly found constitutional republic that would soon morph into the anti-Christ socialist police state we see today. It is this long-standing socialist police state that now has all the American Christians up in arms. Seemingly unbeknownst to Christian Nationalists, democratic socialism is the fate of all constitutional republics. Including the most famous of all, Rome. Which just so happens to be the sixth head of the beast of Revelation 13[2].

Another item rarely acknowledged by Christian Nationalists is that nowhere in the founding documents of the United States does it claim, "Jesus Christ is our Lord and Savior". But rather, they only emphasized "God" in their legal writings. Never once did they write "Lord God" (Jehovah Elohim), nor His only begotten son, "Jesus Christ" (Jehoshua Mashiach) in *any* official document of the state. This is another fact of American history the Christian Nationalists refuse to discuss. They are either willingly ignorant or possess absolutely no insight into the false claims they embrace. How is it possible that the founders of an alleged Christian nation could fail so exclusively to reference even a single instance of Jesus Christ as their King in any legal document?

It will be proven herein how several of the founding fathers blatantly denied the gospel of Jesus Christ. We have letters written by their own hand, recovered, and added to the annals of history[3,15].

Was the United States of America truly founded as a Christian Nation? Or have we *all* been brainwashed into playing a part in the greatest religious hoax of the common era?

Although Christian Nationalism has been a frequent topic of discussion for evangelical historians citing the founding fathers' "Christian roots" (David Barton at Wall Builders,

Hillsdale College, Tony Perkins, Bott radio network, and so on), the fact remains. There has never been a legal precedence for Christianity in any way, shape, or form as the law of the land. In fact, it was quite literally the opposite. The founders wanted to make sure the state could *never* institute a religion by decree. Hence the "freedom of religion" clause is the First Amendment to the constitution.

The politically correct Christian will make statements such as, *"it's freedom of religion, not freedom from religion"*, only to obfuscate the subject matter. Freedom of religion means the state cannot *mandate* a religious practice. That is all. These were the founders' intentions regarding religion and the First Amendment. This means we are *free* from a *forced* religious practice. It means the state is not allowed to force its version of Christianity (or any other religion) on the subject population. What freedom of religion does *not* mean is "this is a Christian nation". That is quite literally the opposite of what it means. In its most basic definition, freedom of religion means you can practice any religious belief you desire. Allow me to repeat that. You can practice any religion you desire...

Now, forget about the founding fathers for a moment. Since when did God the Father or Jesus Christ tell us, *"you have the right to practice any religion you desire. You have freedom of religion"*. Does that sound like a teaching from the gospel of Jesus Christ? Does that sound like something a "Christian nation" would intentionally institute? Does that sound like a plan that is going to turn out well for peace-loving Christians?

No, Christ said, "I am the way, and the truth, and the life; no one comes to the Father except through Me." The more prominent founding fathers of this great nation said *nothing* of the sort, as you will see. The fact is, we are being manipulated and lied to by all the PC Christians on radio, television, and especially those in Washington D.C. And this has all been taking place for a very long time.

On one end of the spectrum, we have people like Donald Trump who use the name "God" frequently and always in as vague a manner as possible. Trump followers are typically the type who don't necessarily care one way or the other if "God" is or is not mentioned in his lengthy political speeches. However, if Trump were to make the unforgivable mistake of stating *"Our Lord Jesus Christ is King of Heaven and Earth, his is the promised Messiah and savior to all mankind"* he would likely lose a vast portion of his supporters instantaneously. Not to mention, his Zionist friends in "Israel" would no longer be pleased with his rhetoric. This may be circumstantial evidence, but it is evidence enough to suggest we are *not* currently a Christian nation, but rather, a nation offering "freedom of religion" where the "God" of your choosing can easily fill in any blanks left vacant by political speeches. Because Trump *is* so crafty with his words, his popularity has become unparalleled in the current political sphere as most Americans do in fact believe in "God".

At the other end of the spectrum, we have people like Andrew Torba and his Gab.com social media and AI platforms rising in popularity. You cannot hear a speech or receive an email from Torba without hearing "Christ is King" at least once. Alex Jones, Sean Hannity, Mark Dice, John Hagee, Robert Jeffress, and countless others fall into this same Christian Nationalist spectrum. Even though they are all at odds with one another on several key Christian doctrines, they are all still serving the same purpose – a militant Christian population who will defend modern Christian doctrines (and modern "Jewish" doctrines) at all costs – including warfare.

Ask yourself, does Christ need our man-made war machines to retain his crown? Have you ever noticed how the nations we defend around the world do not share our Christian faith? Why must we be warmongers in the name of Christ when Christ quite clearly and unobjectionably states in his gospel to practice the opposite?

> Blessed are the peacemakers: for they shall be called the children of God. 10Blessed are they which are persecuted for righteousness' sake: for theirs is the kingdom of heaven. (Matthew 5:9-10)

We can acknowledge it is important to practice self-defense. This will be explained in a moment. But why must we claim that if *we* do not take up arms against our oppressors to "defend the republic" that somehow the gospel of Jesus Christ will cease to exist? How has going to war against our earthly government in the name of "God and Country" become a popular teaching among followers of Christ?

The ideology behind "God and Country" was the same mindset used by the Catholic Pope in the eleventh century when he called for a Crusade to reclaim Jerusalem, to which many of his subjects were happy to oblige. But let's think about this. If Christians were called by God to reclaim Jerusalem from the Muslims on behalf of the Pope, why did the crusades span five centuries? Was Jesus having a difficult time defeating the enemy? No, those crusades were not a commandment of Christ. It is the Lord God who raises nations up and tears them down. Everything else is vanity. If the crusades had been commanded by Christ, or his heavenly Father, they would have been over in a day. When we take it upon ourselves to form our own nations without Christ as the cornerstone, it will be doomed to failure.

Let us now go to the bible to help illustrate this point.

You will be driven away from people and will live with the wild animals; you will eat grass like the ox and be drenched with the dew of heaven. Seven times will pass by for you until you acknowledge that the Most High is sovereign over all kingdoms on earth and gives them to anyone he wishes. (Daniel 4:25; NIV)

Did you know the Christian bible states God himself used the pagan nations to attack Israel when they were found guilty of idolatry? Take a good hard look around. What do you think is happening in this so-called Christian nation of ours?

Therefore, you prostitute, hear the word of the LORD. 36This is what the Lord GOD says: "Because your lewdness was poured out and your nakedness uncovered through your obscene practices with your lovers and with all your detestable idols, and because of the blood of your sons that you gave to idols, 37therefore, behold, I am going to gather all your lovers whom you pleased, all those whom you loved as well as all those whom you hated. So *I will gather them against you from every direction* and expose your nakedness to them so that they may see all your nakedness. 38So I will judge you as women who commit adultery or shed blood are judged; and I will bring on you the blood of wrath and jealousy. 39I will also hand you over to your lovers, and *they will tear down your shrines, demolish your high places,* strip you of your clothing, *take away your jewels,* and will leave you naked and bare. 40*They will incite a crowd against you,* and they will stone you and cut you to pieces with their swords. 41And *they will burn your houses* *with fire* and execute judgments against you in the sight of many women. Then I will put an end to your prostitution, and you will also no longer pay your lovers. 42So I will satisfy My fury against you and My jealousy will leave you, and I will be pacified and no longer be angry. 43Since you have not remembered the days of your youth but have caused Me unrest by all these things, behold, I in turn will bring your conduct down on your own head," declares the Lord GOD, "so that you will not commit this outrageous sin in addition to all your other abominations. (Ezekiel 16:35-43; NAS)

Christ does not need our help in defeating the enemies of God, nor do the Father's prophecies regarding war in the end times need Christian assistance to come to fruition. God is in control, and we are not. The reason Christian Nationalists cannot see these simple truths is that they are unwilling to peacefully humble themselves before Christ and our heavenly Father. They are either unwilling or unable to comprehend the Father's perfect law of love. A love that we Americans have feigned and perverted.

God used the pagan nations to "destroy utterly" those among Israel who were using His name inappropriately. This is mentioned several times throughout the Old Testament. God will tear down *His* own people, the people who claim to be *His* nation, and *He* will use the pagan nations surrounding them to accomplish *His* will. Is any of this starting to sound familiar?

Trump and Torba were used as examples in this chapter because they are both prominent figures in the Christian Nationalist Movement and frankly, they are easy targets. Unfortunately, there are many more leading public figures who possess this same heinous pride plaguing our Christian population.

The ideologies of Trump and Torba are similar in nature regarding national identity but differ in the origin of their alleged authority to make such bold statements. For instance, Donald Trump claims "God" gives us the power to harness our freedom without ever once mentioning to which "God" he is referring. *Exactly* like the "founding fathers" wrote in their Declaration of Independence. Meanwhile, Andrew Torba claims "Christ is King" gives us the power and freedom necessary to fight the good fight by any means necessary – including warfare.

Certain similarities between what Paul described nearly 2000 years ago and what we are witnessing today in the Christian Nationalist movements are uncanny.

> 12 What I mean is this: One of you says, "I follow Paul"; another, "I follow Apollos"; another, "I follow Cephas"; still another, "I follow Christ." 13 Is Christ divided? Was Paul crucified for you? Were you baptized in the name of Paul? 14 I thank God that I did not baptize any of you except Crispus and Gaius. (1 Corinthians 1:12-14; NIV)

Do you hear, "I follow Donald Trump", "I follow Mark Dice", "I follow Ron Desantis", "I follow Andrew Torba", "I follow Alex Jones" "I follow John Hagee" or "I follow Jesus Christ", on and on, and on. None of these Christian Nationalist movements are following the teachings of Jesus Christ but are indeed following a Christ of their own design.

Everyone loses when we use God's name inappropriately. And every Christian will lose when we try to take up arms in the name of Christ. It is not the duty of a Christian to dethrone an earthly king, or an earthly politician. It is God

Himself who brings nations up and tears them down. Trust in God. Have faith in His only begotten son, Jesus Christ. This is what matters. Who wins the next election, who wins the next war, or who will be in power by the time *you* accomplish such and such, does not matter at all. Obedience is the only thing that matters. Faith is the only thing that will bring us through difficult times, global terror, and especially persecution for His name's sake.

Eternal life is waiting for us in the name of the precious son of God. Christ himself said his kingdom is somewhere else... what exactly are we defending in this dying world?

> Daniel answered and said, Blessed be the name of God for ever and ever: for wisdom and might are his: 21 And he changeth the times and the seasons: *he removeth kings, and setteth up kings*: he giveth wisdom unto the wise, and knowledge to them that know understanding: 22 He revealeth the deep and secret things: he knoweth what is in the darkness, and the light dwelleth with him. (Daniel 2:20-22)

> But God is the judge: he putteth down one, and setteth up another. (Psalm 75:7)

> Dearly beloved, avenge not yourselves, but rather give place unto wrath: for it is written, Vengeance is mine; I will repay, saith the Lord. (Romans 12:19)

While the majority in these movements play politics by casting their ballot in federal elections leaving the rest to democracy, there are others who are aggressively pushing to influence a new type of Christian Nationalism. This new ideology is convincing people that since our federal government is corrupt beyond measure, which is true, we need to start reclaiming cities and towns at the grassroots level; local governments, local school boards, and our local economic prosperity by manufacturing locally and buying locally, grow our own food locally and stop eating manufactured garbage (all of which is also true), but to the central point of this chapter, they believe we should form local militias to go to war with anyone who disagrees with Christ. Including our federal government. And for those who wish to attack us from around the world, we *must* go to war, even in our own communities, if we are to defend Christ's values in *his* homeland – the USA. After all, it is *he* who founded "the greatest nation on earth," is it not? So, in that case, why wouldn't *he* want *us* to defend *his* country by any means necessary? That is Christian Nationalism (a.k.a. Christian deism) in a nutshell.

Visual representations of this ideology can be found all over the internet. There is a famous picture of a parade being led by a man holding a flag declaring, "Christ is my Savior – Trump is my President". Another flag exclusively found on Gab.com has an Eagle with its wings spread, a bible strapped to the eagle's chest, a Roman cross grasped by one talon with an AR-15 clutched in the other. Naturally, the banner atop the eagle shows the Latin phrase "Logos Lux" meaning in English, "words of light". That's right… forget about the gospel of Jesus Christ. The new "words of light" belong to Andrew Torba.

Now, there's no reason to be "anti-gun", and every reason to be pro-self-defense. But since when did the followers of Christ need Abrams tanks, stealth aircraft, and nuclear weapons to preach the gospel? Let's get real. Modern souls are once again being deceived by Satan while using the name of "God" (the likes of Trump) and "Christ is King" (the likes of Torba) as the springboard for their movements.

Only Christ can deliver our people from bondage. Yet, the majority still clings to their preferred politician, businessman, or favorite denomination as if any one of them can deliver their souls from the unsalvageable mess of this so-called constitutional republic. It is time to wake up to reality and accept the fact that no matter what happens next, Christ is still on his throne.

~

In the book of Ezekiel, we read of a hard-hearted people who were professing the name of the One True God while seeking the desires of their own manmade idols, lusts, and allegiances. God had forsaken the people of Israel and Judah for committing idolatries in His name. What happened next forever changed Israel, Judah, and their relationship with the world.

It is time for the Christian Nationalist movement to learn specifically what God does with those who claim to be *His* people while using *His* name inappropriately. It is time to learn what happens when "one nation under God" begins using God's name and God's commandments in vain. What are God's promises to *His* people?

> And the LORD said to him, "Go through the midst of the city, through the midst of Jerusalem, and make a mark on the foreheads of the people who groan and sigh over all the abominations which are being committed in its midst." 5But to the others He said in my presence, "Go through the city after him and strike; do not let your eye have pity and do not spare. 6Utterly kill old men, young

men, female virgins, little children, and women, but do not touch any person on whom is the mark; and you shall start from My sanctuary." So they started with the elders who were before the temple. 7He also said to them, "Defile the temple and fill the courtyards with the dead. Go out!" So they went out and struck and killed the people in the city. 8And as they were striking the people and I alone was left, I fell on my face and cried out, saying, "Oh, Lord GOD! Are You going to destroy the entire remnant of Israel by pouring out Your wrath on Jerusalem?" 9Then He said to me, "The guilt of the house of Israel and Judah is very, very great, and the land is filled with blood, and the city is full of perversion; for they say, 'The LORD has abandoned the land, and the LORD does not see!' (Ezekiel 9:4-9; NAS)

The only people who were spared from God's wrath were the ones who wept over the abominations taking place in His name. The Christian Nationalists should take heed of this warning. All Judeans who went to war against Nebuchadnezzar's pagan forces (forces which were sent by God Himself; Daniel 4:25; Ezekiel 9; 16) were either killed or forced into exile because they did not have "the mark" of God *in* their forehead.

In the time of Ezekiel, the house of Judah was found pursuing the gods of the surrounding territories because Jehovah was no longer speaking to them directly. They were willing to seek a presence with "God" by any means available to them. This is a considerably dumbed-down statement, but for lack of a better phrase that is exactly what took place.

For the sake of the modern United States, we likewise have chosen to defend our "Christian country" with its many lukewarm Christ-like religions by any means available to *us*. As true Christianity slowly fades into obscurity, we subconsciously give rise to the Christian Nationalist movement. It is now justified to think that if Christ is not coming back to fix this mess himself, he *must* have meant it is up to *us* to defend *his* honor and protect our Christian republic (this ideology is known as Christian Deism, explained thoroughly in chapter four). To do so, we sift through the printed words of the prophets, and those of Christ and his apostles looking for any reason to go to war to defend our homeland (explained thoroughly in chapter two). All the while the same idolatries and perversions taking place in ancient Israel are taking place right here and now as a result of "freedom of religion".

Ezekiel 9:9 shown above sounds an awful lot like the warnings given by Jesus' apostles. Jesus told Peter that in the last days, people would "scoff" at the prophecies claiming Christ has taken too long to return or is not coming back. As a result, they would take matters into their own hands.

> Then He said to me, "The guilt of the house of Israel and Judah is very, very great, and the land is filled with blood, and the city is full of perversion; for they say, *'The LORD has abandoned the land,* and the LORD does not see!' (Ezekiel 9:9; NAS)

> Know this first of all, that in the last days mockers will come with their mocking, following after their own lusts, 4and saying, *"Where is the promise of His coming?* For ever since the fathers fell asleep, all things continue just as they were from the beginning of creation." (2 Peter 3:3-4; NAS)

> But you, beloved, ought to remember the words that were spoken beforehand by the apostles of our Lord Jesus Christ, 18that they were saying to you, "In the last time there will

be mockers, following after their own ungodly lusts." *19These are the ones who cause divisions, worldly-minded, devoid of the Spirit.* (Jude 17-19; NAS)

The spiritual visions and historical events recorded in the book of Ezekiel were at a time when Judah had been taken captive by Nebuchadnezzar's forces into Babylon. And if you recall, not all the Judeans were taken. Some were left behind. With those who were left behind, there appears to have been a rift. Some failed to change their ways while others cried with sorrow for the destruction of Jerusalem. Those who knew Israel and Judah had been committing fornication with other gods were spared. It is these people who were left living in the land after Judah's captivity, later to flee the territory alive. It is these people who were "marked" *in* their foreheads with a sign that only the angels could see. They were spared from annihilation because they had not practiced idolatry at the heights of Jerusalem's greatness. God saved the people who had "the mark in their forehead" (sound familiar? Revelation 14:1-5) because they wept and prayed for forgiveness while their brothers and sisters were committing idolatry in the land of Judea.

So… we have now come back full circle. *If* the United States of America is indeed a country founded by Christ and his heavenly Father, we would be wise to repent and avoid the idolatries taking place in His name, wouldn't we? We would be wise to mourn for the loss of souls and not diminish ourselves to the standards of politically correct Christianity, wouldn't we? If we really are "one nation under God" then by all biblical measures, God is in control, and He is no doubt full of wrath for what America has become. We should return to the Most High God and His *right*eousness while keeping faith that His will be done in our land (for better or worse). And if we fail to repent as a nation, God will eventually "kill utterly" all those who practice abominations in His name, while those who have His mark/seal "in their foreheads" may very well be left behind to inherit the land.

This is the way it happened during the time of the flood. Noah and his family were the only people spared. This is the way it happened in the time of Sodom and Gomorrah. Lot and his family were the only people spared. This is the way it happened in Egypt. Those who sprinkled the blood of the lamb on their doorposts were the only people "passed over", they were the only people spared. This is the way it happened in Jerusalem (Ezekiel 9), those who wept for righteousness' sake were the only people spared. Over, and over, and over. This apparently is the way God works. Only those who accept his *right*eousness as a gift are spared and left behind to inherit the land. In the end of days, those who seek God's *right*eousness will have been "left behind" one last time. This time, they will be left behind for a thousand-year reign of Christ after the first resurrection (Revelation 20:4-5). Just like Jesus prophesied, "blessed are the meek, they will inherit the earth." (Matthew 5:5) More on that topic in the next book in this series, "The Rapture Delusion."

~

The Christian Nationalists love quoting the bible to furnish their arguments. While debating them online, I have come across the same two Jesus quotes over, and over, and over. It's as if they exist in an echo chamber where nobody has ever bothered to study these bible passages for themselves. We will now address these two most popular quotes

Christian Political Correctness

of Jesus before traversing any farther down the rabbit hole. Their go-to quote from our Lord is found in Luke 22:36.

> Then said he unto them, But now, he that hath a purse, let him take it, and likewise his scrip: and he that hath no sword, let him sell his garment, and buy one. (Luke 22:36)

To illustrate this common perception, I will add a direct conversation posted on Gab.com where I was debating one of the many Christian Nationalist followers. For the sake of this man's anonymity, we will refer to him only as Mr. Sasquatch (he prefers this title). In the conversation below, the comments of Mr. Sasquatch will be shown in *italics* to differentiate between his speech and mine.

You opened by asking, *"So sell your cloak and buy a sword what does it really mean?"*

In saying this, Jesus was fulfilling yet another prophecy from Isaiah. Jesus needed to be "numbered with the transgressors". The act of having that sword, at that specific moment in time, was worthy for Christ to be "numbered with the transgressors". It was a fulfillment of prophecy, not a call to arms and warfare in the name of God, such as the jihadists.

> "Now, however," He told them, "the one with a purse should take it, and likewise a bag; and the one without a sword should sell his cloak and buy one. 37For I tell you that this Scripture must be fulfilled in Me: '**And He was numbered with the transgressors**.' For what is written about Me is reaching its fulfillment." 38So they said, "Look, Lord, here are two swords." "That is

enough," He answered. (Luke 22:36-38; BSB; emphasis mine throughout)

Too many Christians use Luke 22:36 to suggest we must all "purchase swords" and go to war in the name of Jesus. How do we not understand the context leading up to, and following these texts? Why must people so blatantly take this and other verses out of context to suit their vengeful appetites? Have you ever noticed how people will quote verse 36, but they will NEVER talk about verses 37 and 38 which state in Jesus' own words that the only reason he said this specific statement "buy a sword" was to fulfill the scripture, which as any objective scholar would know is pointing to Isaiah 53:12 – a fulfillment of prophecy. Not a call to action and warfare in Jesus' name.

> "Therefore will I divide him a portion with the great, and he shall divide the spoil with the strong; because he hath poured out his soul unto death: and *he was numbered with the transgressors*; and he bare the sin of many, and made intercession for the transgressors." (Isaiah 53:12)

You may notice this unanimous conclusion in the footnotes of your bible. In Luke 22:36-38, Jesus was referring to Isaiah 53:12. Jesus specifically said this in his own words (Luke 22:37). Read the whole chapter in context with the prophecy Jesus is referring to.

He was numbered with the transgressors... why did Jesus tell them to purchase swords? To allow the Romans to falsely accuse Jesus of being a transgressor when we all know he was anything but that. Because it is likely that he (Jesus) would have foreknown Peter would try to defend him by attacking the guards (the same way Jesus knew Peter would deny him three times before the rooster crowed), he told Peter and his immediate followers (not you and I), to purchase a sword knowing full well Peter would attack that soldier, leading to Jesus and his peaceful followers being accused of transgressions. Transgressions that fulfilled the prophecy in Isaiah 53.

Notice also how Peter did not get arrested that night. Even after trying to kill a Roman soldier, only Jesus was arrested... I find that very interesting.

Further, why did Jesus then immediately tell Peter, "Put down your sword, or you will die by the sword"? Why? Because the prophecy had in that very moment been fulfilled! Jesus then healed the soldier's head wound and told Peter to put down his sword. Jesus could now go to the cross as a transgressor even though he was innocent. Exactly as the prophecies foretold.

The Christian Nationalists do not like talking about the fact that Jesus told Peter to put down the sword (yes, the very same sword he so recently told them to purchase). It nullifies their argument at point blank. Which is why they *only* quote Luke 22:36 and *none* of the rest of the chapter.

> You then asked, *"When Peter cut the ear off the Roman did Jesus rebuke him for cutting his ear off and tell him to get rid of that weapon of war?"*

Yes, that is exactly what Jesus did. Read Luke 22 in its entirety. Read it carefully and deliberately. Not in soundbites posted on social media.

This is speculation on my part, but Mr. Sasquatch's question sounds as if he was trying to trick me, hoping I had never read Luke 22 for myself. *"why didn't Jesus rebuke Peter then, huh?"*. Well, in fact, Jesus did rebuke Peter. So, either Mr. Sasquatch was trying to trick me, or he had never read Luke 22 himself and was just another victim of the Satanic echo chambers on Gab.com spinning false doctrine for the politically correct Christian movements.

> 38So they said, "Look, Lord, here are two swords." "That is enough," He answered." (Luke 22:38; BSB)

Why would Christ say, "that is enough" to the comment about the disciples having only two swords? Are two swords enough to defend against the Roman legions? Of course not. Going to war in Jesus' name was never the intention of Jesus' statement in verse 36. However, two swords **are** enough to attack a soldier and be counted among the transgressors. Which is the sole purpose of Jesus' statements in Luke 22.

> You then asked, *Additionally, why were the disciplines armed in the first place?*

First of all, what makes you think the apostles and disciples were walking around armed like soldiers? That's not what it says, not anywhere in the NT. (At most, they possessed two swords. Or, as Jesus said, they needed to go buy swords to fulfill the prophecy. Remember Matthew 10? "These twelve Jesus sent out with the following instructions: Do not go among the Gentiles or enter any town of the Samaritans. 6Go rather to the lost sheep of Israel. 7As you go, proclaim this message: 'The kingdom of heaven has come near.' 8Heal the sick, raise the dead, cleanse those who have leprosy, a drive out demons. Freely you have received; freely give. 9"*Do not get any gold or silver or copper to take with you in your belts – 10no bag for the journey or extra shirt or sandals or a staff, for the worker is worth his keep.*" They were told to go out into the country with *nothing*.)

But, for argument's sake, let's say all the apostles and disciples were armed to the teeth (which they were not). There is nothing wrong with arming yourself in self-defense. For instance, if a rabid dog attacks a child, that dog should be put down. The dog is mentally and physically incapable of having peaceful interactions with human beings. That dog has made its decision to be vicious. For whatever reason, domestication, disease, whatever, that dog is no longer a blessing to the Lord. The Lord our God will not frown upon us putting a rabid dog down if it has come to the point of mindlessly killing anyone it can sink its teeth into. That is self-defense. Now, does this mean we are permitted to take it upon ourselves as followers of Christ to travel the world killing each dog that we deem to be a threat or a possible threat? No, it does not. We as men and women can defend ourselves when an event arises, even with lethal force if required, but only when it is in self-defense. To further this illustration, let's take the Aurora Colorado theater shooting as an example. If there were an armed citizen at the entrance to that theater when the gunman entered the room, said citizen could have saved many lives that day. The shooter had already made his decision to enter the pits of hell by doing the will of Satan. He had become an unsalvageable rabid dog, and the person with a single pistol and a single bullet could have ended that tragedy before it had begun. That is self-defense. A defense for the common good. The man acting in self-defense for the people in that theater would not have been a murderer. He would have saved some 70 otherwise innocent lives that day. He would have been a hero. But, again, that does not give Christians the right to travel the globe saying, "we are going to war in the name of Christ because you will eventually try to kill us!" Can you see? There is a difference between self-defense against a rabid dog and making a conscious preemptive effort to go to war in the name of Jesus Christ, or "God" to "reclaim the Holy Land", or whatever your intentions are. Do we think God needs our help to reclaim something that already belongs to Him? If you do, you have never read the bible. And as far as telling Peter and the apostles to *"sell your cloak and buy a sword"*, that was a deliberate act by Jesus to fulfill one more prophecy of Isaiah 53 before intentionally going to the cross. Innocence – to be numbered among the transgressors.

You also mentioned ***If it be possible****, as much as lieth in you, live peaceably with all men." Romans 12:18 To live peaceably with all men **goes without saying** that the "men" are peaceful as well. Also, **do you even know the definition of "meek"** apparently you don't "Mild of temper; soft; gentle; not easily provoked or irritated; yielding; given to forbearance under injuries." 1828 Dictionary. You know who the dictionary uses as an example, Moses, **did Moses not lead men to battle?** Words have meaning not easily provoked or irritated, or yielding this would also be supported by "Wherefore, my beloved brethren, let every man be swift to hear, slow to speak, slow to wrath" James*

1:19 Slow to anger is important but it does not say never be angry, there is a time for that as well!

My response to that is I would be happy to send you a free copy of my second book, *The Evil God of Love*. I have written thoughtfully about the topic of God leading people into battle. By the way, you are using an atheist argument to counter my points, just FYI for awareness. And why would you assume I don't know the definition of meek? You know what they say about assumptions.

In the *full* conversation (not listed), Mr. Sasquatch and his fellow soldiers were anything but meek. He then proceeds to chastise me about not being meek (in his own words *"Mild of temper; soft; gentle; not easily provoked or irritated; yielding; given to forbearance under injuries"*) while at the same time claiming we should go to war with those who disagree with Christ. The double standard offered by the Christian Nationalists on the right is very similar to their opponents on the left. Our interaction reminded me of a metaphor my wife told me recently. "Right-wing, left-wing; two wings of the same bird."

Mr. Sasquatch also mentioned, *"To live peaceably with all men goes without saying that the "men" are peaceful as well"*. No, it does not "go without saying" because that is an open-ended statement. What he *is* saying is that we should only be peaceful with peaceful men. And we should reserve the right to be hawkish with hawkish men. So, if a man is not peaceful with me, my actions would be *right*eous to punch him in the nose. *They* are not peaceful therefore *I* am not required to be peaceful. This, among many others, is a prime example of twisting scripture to suit an agenda because "it goes without saying" that Paul did not mean peaceful, he meant hawkish.

And we can dismiss Christ's message as well when he said, "blessed are the peacemakers" (Matthew 5:9).

Paul also made the comment *"If it be possible"* to be peaceful with all men. This could very well be Paul alluding to self-defense. Remember how Jesus told us to turn the other cheek?

> "You have heard that it was said, 'AN EYE FOR AN EYE, AND A TOOTH FOR A TOOTH [punishment that fits the offense].' 39But I say to you, do not resist an evil person [who insults you or violates your rights]; but whoever [l] slaps you on the right cheek, turn the other toward him also [simply ignore insignificant insults or trivial losses and do not bother to retaliate--maintain your dignity, your self-respect, your poise]. 40If anyone wants to sue you and take your shirt, [m]let him have your coat also [for the Lord repays the offender]. 41And whoever [n]forces you to go one mile, go with him two. 42Give to him who asks of you, and do not turn away from him who wants to borrow from you." (Matthew 5:38-42; AMP)

Christ was clearly talking about revenge – "an eye for an eye". We should not take revenge because vengeance belongs to God. We already know this from several additional scriptures. But does that mean when we are actively being attacked by a rabid dog, we are not allowed to attempt to stop the dog from ripping into our flesh? Being persecuted because we preach a righteous doctrine is one thing, we should proclaim the truth even if it means the end of our current flesh life. But being attacked by a rabid dog who cares nothing about our doctrine nor has any idea who we are or what purpose we serve is another thing altogether.

The dog doesn't know any better, and I would like to save my leg from amputation, please.

Let us consider this carefully. If someone punches me in the face, do I punch him back? Well, why was he punching me? Did he punch me as a result of the doctrine I was peacefully preaching? Or did he run into a crowd with a machete randomly attacking innocent women and children at the point when I was hit? Common sense can go a long way. Why was I punched? Why was someone attacking me? Is my response self-defense, or revenge after the fact? Was anyone's life in jeopardy? If no, then at that point, I would be practicing revenge by "punching them back", not self-defense.

Let's take this analogy a step further. If someone punches me in the face, I then turn my cheek to allow him to strike me again (if he is still so angry at me). In doing so, I could in theory use this opportunity to witness peace and how God is in control. Vengeance belongs to God, and I will not succumb to fighting just because you are angry with me. Now that I have seared this man's conscience with the truth, my witness for Christ is made known. The seed has been planted. The Holy Spirit is now at work whether for or against that individual.

Again, taking the analogy one step further. This man is now consumed with great fury that I have invoked the name of our Lord, he turns his attention to my toddler son. He begins assaulting my toddler son with his fists. Do I stand idle and say, "*son, you must turn the other cheek. Do not return violence with violence, son. Come on now, son, you can take it, hang in there... He'll probably stop beating you soon. It's okay, I have faith that everything will work out according to God's plan. Just hang in there, boy. It is God's will that we turn the other cheek.*" I **could** say that... but I am **not** going to stand by idle. So, what do I do as the man continues beating my baby boy to death? Is *that* turning the other cheek? Or is that an accomplice to murder when I had every chance to stop the murder while it was actively taking place? Is that what Christ intended when asking us to turn the other cheek? To allow senseless unprovoked murder to take place in front of our eyes? Is that what Paul intended when telling us to live peaceably with all men? No, at that point you would be an accomplice to attempted murder if you did not stop that man from beating a defenseless child to death.

There is a difference between "turning the other cheek" and defending innocent life against the attack of a rabid dog. You can quote me on that.

To understand this scripture, I have employed basic logic, reason, and common sense. I am not twisting scripture. I am allowing the scripture to remain pure while using my knowledge of *all* scripture to divide the word of truth.

We need to call these people out for quoting a single bible verse without giving any additional context of any kind. Scriptural or otherwise.

Mr. Sasquatch used Romans 12:18 to attack my position, but he failed to quote the surrounding statements in the same chapter.

> Do not be wise in your own estimation. 17Never pay back evil for evil to anyone. Respect what is right in the sight of all men. 18*If possible*, so far as it depends on you, be at peace with all men. 19*Never take your own revenge*, beloved, but leave room for the wrath of God, for it is written, "VENGEANCE IS MINE, I WILL REPAY," says the Lord. (Romans 12:16-19; NAS)

Their tactic is employed by quoting a single sentence from the bible immediately before flooding the conversation with hours of politically correct soundbites, memes, and links to other sites. It becomes quite difficult to refute these claims in real-time when there are five or ten social media warriors attacking you all at once. How do you answer all of them, all at the same time?

One of the faithful Christian Nationalist warriors once asked me, *"why don't you just write a book about it and tell us all how we're so wrong"* ... well, I tried, but none whom I have spoken with are willing to accept the free literature at their disposal.

Notice specifically verse 19 (Romans 12) which states "never take your own revenge". Can we admit there is a difference between taking revenge and defending ourselves against the attack of a wild animal?

We should return to the Aurora Colorado Theater shooting analogy for another example. Consider the innocent man concealing a self-defense pistol seated by the door near where the shooter entered the room and opened fire. He could have stopped the shooter immediately, saving many lives that day. That is self-defense. This could very well be the "If at all possible" Paul was referring to in the verse Sasquatch quoted. But what if the shooter spotted and killed the would-be hero before he had the opportunity to save those seventy lives? Well, he and everyone else would have still died that day.

Now imagine the would-be hero had a devout and loving brother. This brother has become filled with unfathomable rage. This brother then tracks down every living relative of the shooter's family to return the favor by killing them all in cold blood. That is called revenge. One is lawful, the other is not. There is a difference between self-defense (stopping the shooter in action) and revenge (killing the shooter's whole family after the fact). That is what the "Christian" Nationalists don't understand.

We don't want our small child to be attacked by a rabid dog, nor do we want to put the dog down. But in the event the child is attacked, and killed, we cannot, in turn, kill the dog's owners, and the owner's whole family in revenge. That is unlawful in the eyes of God. There is no *right*eousness in that.

Moving on to Mr. Sasquatch's comment about Moses leading people to battle, I offered him a free copy of the book, *the Evil God of Love*[4], to which he declined. If he had read it, he would recall the reason God led the infant nation of Israel into battle was to prepare the territory for the coming of the Messiah. It was through the tribe of Judah that the Messiah would be born. The pagan nations standing in God's way were wicked beyond belief. Not to mention, God knew them before they were born (Ezekiel 28-31). They had already made their decision to follow Satan long ago. And so, to make way for the Messiah, the LORD God took them out of the picture.

Atheists use these biblical scenarios to suggest God "committed genocide" upon an entire race of people. As irony (and hypocrisy) would have it, these same people had previously committed "genocide" upon others. How else would they have occupied the land? How does anyone, ever, in the history of the world, occupy a land without warfare, bloodshed, or "genocide" upon the local inhabitants? This is true even in the United States of America. Did the American government ask the native population to peacefully move west on the trail of tears? No, they did not. Did the Egyptians, the Assyrians, the Babylonians, the Medes, the Persians, did the Romans ever ask politely? No, they murdered, pillaged, and raped their way into the land just like everyone else.

That is why God "led Mosses into battle" as Mr. Sasquatch claims. To make way for the Messiah. But, here's the kicker. Now that the Messiah *has* come, there is no longer a need for God to lead his people (followers of Christ – spiritual Israel) into battle. The battle is already won, and the enemy was defeated at the cross! That's the difference!

The treatise above would have been my response to Mr. Sasquatch, but he soon retreated from the conversation, and I have not heard back from him since.

Satan has always sought to kill God's prophets. When Satan made the ignorant mistake of killing God's only begotten son (innocent blood, shed for the sins of mankind), he signed and sealed his own death warrant once and for all.

In summary, the Christian Nationalists use Luke 22:36 to promote war in the name of Christ, and never do they quote anything other than verse 36. If they do, their argument is shown for what it is. Easily avoidable ignorance.

~

The second verse the Christian Nationalists love to quote is found in the tenth chapter of Matthew.

> Think not that I am come to send peace on earth: I came not to send peace, but a sword. (Matthew 10:34)

The most obvious aspect of their flawed thinking is found in the quote itself. Jesus said "I" will send a sword. What Jesus did not say is, "I am sending *you* out with swords to attack anyone who will not receive my gospel message." Which is literally what the Christian Nationalists are claiming. In fact, Jesus said the exact opposite only a moment earlier in the same conversation (Matthew 10:9-10).

The second aspect is knowing the definition of Jesus' "sword" in scripture. The sword Jesus Christ is referring to is the Word of God (Revelation 19:15-21), not literally a physical sword. Jesus spoke in parables.

The third point which should also be obvious, is that Jesus never went around attacking people with a sword. Nor did his followers ever attack people with swords based on Christ's teachings (except for that one time with Peter... already explained). Clearly, "the sword" is symbolism pointing to something else. And, as mentioned, we know this metaphor is referring to the word of God that will smite the rebellious nations (God will have His vengeance, not us). It is the word of God that can cut into a person's heart and pierce their soul. That is the "sword" Jesus is referring to.

Remember how all of creation, **and** the coming judgement, proceeds forth from the "word of God" (John 1; 2 Peter 3:13; Revelation 21). The word of God proceeding forth from the mouth of Jesus; that is "the sword".

One final item to address. The Christian Nationalists will claim protecting The United States from the onslaught at the border (illegal immigration) is in fact self-defense. Or that going to war with our government is justified to defend the constitution of our Christian homeland via our Second Amendment Rights. They will claim that defending a nation or a "homeland" from invaders is synonymous with defending against a "rabid dog". They could turn my Aurora Colorado shooter analogy back on me by saying, "we are practicing self-defense by defending our country the same way the would-be hero was defending the theater", but... listen...

If this *is* a Christian nation, and if this *is* God's country, and we **are** God's people, then according to the way God works in the bible, he is very unhappy with us. Why else would God send an onslaught to attack His nation at every level; physically, socially, economically, politically, and religiously?

What exactly can we do to defend against a divine onslaught... go to war with God? If so, that is not self-defense. That is suicide by standing up to your creator in vain. Exactly like the Jews did in the time of the Babylonian exile (read the book of Ezekiel).

We would be wise to do as the minority did during the Babylonian exile. Repent and mourn for the sins taking place in our great nation.

~

There are only two ways to look at these claims objectively.

First, is the idea that we *are* a nation under God. And since God does not change who He is, we'd better change who we are, and fast! By the looks of the political, social, and religious norms in the United States of America, it is far too late for the whole flock to be saved. Can you envision an entire nation of people as diverse as the USA all fasting in prayer and repentance at the same time? This will never happen. But for individuals across the country and across the world, we still have time to repent. We always have time to repent. Every single day.

Second, is the idea that we are *not* a nation under God, and we never were. Which would mean we are all on our own in defending what is left of this so-called constitutional republic.

Whether we choose to believe option one or option two, the wise among us will peer through the veil to see a third option. Repentance. It is time to repent and get right with

God *personally* before it is too late. I for one am taking advantage of this knowledge and I pray you do as well.

More detail is offered in the coming chapters, but for now, I leave you with this thought. We should beware of any Christian who uses a singular verse to prove their theology, their personal beliefs, and especially their political agenda. If you find the opportunity to talk to a devout Christian Nationalist yourself, ask them if they can offer **any** scriptures from the New Testament, in Jesus's own words, that promote the warfare they desire. Chances are, you'll now be able to stop them dead in their tracks when they inevitably quote Matthew 10 or Luke 22.

The Bible is a rather large book. Perhaps we should read it through and through for confirmation before taking a stand.

As Ronald Ragan used to say, "Trust, but verify". Rather, we should argue; **trust** in the Lord Jesus Christ, and *verify* the people quoting soundbite scripture are not ravenous wolves in sheep's clothing, thirsting for their next taste of blood.

CHAPTER 2

PERSECUTION AND FIGHTING BACK

"Upon my return from the army to Baltimore in the winter of 1777, I sat next to John Adams in Congress, and upon my whispering to him and asking him if he thought we should succeed in our struggle with Great Britain, he answered me, "Yes-if we fear God and repent of our sins."
~ Benjamin Rush
(Pennsylvania delegate to the Continental Congress)

As a young American Christian, I once believed a devout tyrant named King George III had been persecuting our forefathers for practicing their religion in a way that conflicted with his own. I had assumed this religious dispute was a defining factor in the American Revolution and the war for independence, and I had likely made this assumption by knowing the First Amendment to the Constitution states, "Congress shall make no law respecting an establishment of religion or prohibiting the free exercise thereof". To my knowledge, this portion of the First Amendment was a revolutionary response to King George III attempting to institute a tyrannical state-sponsored religion in North America. Why else would the authors make the issue of religion and free speech the first defining point in their constitution if someone, somewhere, were not forcing their beliefs on others?

I cannot recall how or why I adopted this thinking, but all the pieces of the puzzle did seem to fit. Looking back, I now understand this unwitting departure from historical truth was based on my sheer lack of knowledge. I was ignorant of the facts.

The evidence, however, would lead me in a direction opposed to my former assumptions. Persecution of Christians taking place in the new world was not the result of the Anglican church under the king's authority, but rather, a colonial offshoot and divestiture from the Church of England that George III had no part in orchestrating or promoting.

> The Declaration of Independence casts George III as the leading villain of the American Revolution. It asserts that he was a prince whose character was "marked by every act which may define a Tyrant" and pronounces him "unfit to be the ruler of a free people." As a member of the original committee that drafted the Declaration of Independence, John Adams later admitted that it contains "expressions which I would not have inserted, if I had drawn it up, particularly that which called the King tyrant." Reminiscing at the age of eighty-eight, Adams thought it "too personal ... too passionate, and too much like scolding, for so grave and solemn a document." He confessed that he "never believed George to be a tyrant" or to be guilty of the "cruel" *acts committed in the name of the King*. In his autobiography,

Adams was also critical of Benjamin Franklin for his "severe resentment" and personal animosity towards George III. According to Adams, regardless of the appropriateness of the occasion, Franklin never missed an opportunity to cast aspersions upon George III.[5] (emphasis mine)

"Acts committed in the name of the King", not "by the order of the King".

Here is the truth. If I kill someone in the name of Christ, it does not mean Christ ordered me to kill that person. It means I am a delusional psychopath who took it upon myself, under my own cognizance, to commit murder. It is true that George III was harsh toward his subjects when he needed to be. But to the extent, some believe George III was responsible for religious persecution in the thirteen colonies, this is simply not true. It would be more truthful to suggest the current situation in the United States of America far surpasses any religious tyranny George III promoted during his tenure as King of England.

If George III was not the iron hand behind the persecution of early American Christians, who was?

> Europe had experienced many wars from the time of Constantine through the Reformation era on down to the time in which this generation of Christians lived who had settled in the American Colonies. Many of those wars had seen professing Christians fighting and killing one another. These people [*Quakers and Anabaptists*] wanted no part of killing anyone, but especially not their fellow Christians. This would be a betrayal to their Lord in their eyes. (emphasis mine throughout)

> When the Revolutionary War broke out in 1776, many Americans were ready to stand up and fight for their freedoms. After all, they had been resisting **British taxation** and enforcement thereof for more than a decade. But not all Americans were in favor of war in order to solve their problems. In fact, there were some groups of devout Christians who would rather die than take the sword. In particular among these were the Quakers and those we know as the Anabaptists (Amish, Mennonites, Brethren, etc.). These Christians went against the grain of the dominant thinking patterns of their day. Moreover, they paid a high price for it. In the process of refusing to resist evil, these peace-loving Christians were met with severe persecution from their patriotic neighbors. In the process of defending what they believed were their freedoms by divine right, the Colonists, in their treatment of these Christians, tyrannically deprived their peaceful neighbors of some of those necessary freedoms in order to gain their own.[6]

The picture painted above is a near mirror image of the Christian Nationalist movement growing in America today. When debating them online, they have warned me on more than one occasion that I (a peace-loving Christian) am part of the problem and need to "get out of the way" if I am not willing to "man up" and defend my homeland. This is a delicate way of saying they are willing to force peaceful Christians "out of the way" when the war drums begin pounding on American soil once again.

It is quite clear when looking back at the historical record that the persecution taking place against Christians in the American colonies was not propagated by George III but was a result of the colonial settlers infighting amongst themselves. It would appear to be no different in the twenty-first century. Christians are willing to persecute other Christians if they don't "get out of the way" or "man up" in an effort to prepare for a new American revolution.

To be clear, the early Christian settlers were being persecuted by other Christian settlers, and never were they persecuted under the direction of George III. That persecution would come later only as a result of money and taxation, *not* Christian doctrine. The Christian persecution taking place in the colonies was a homegrown grassroots conquest over who would be the more dominant party. One perfect illustration of this conflict can be found in the history of a group known as the Puritans.

Those in the Puritan sect were fiercely loyal to the crown of King Henry VIII, even centuries later. Their creation was a result of Henry VIII parting ways with the Catholic Church during the time of the Reformation in the sixteenth century. After the split from Rome, the English dynasty would possess total authority over religious affairs throughout Great Britain, dismissing the Pope's long-standing reign over church doctrine. The Puritans would grow to be as harsh to the dissenters of the Anglican Church as the Catholics were to the dissenters of Catholicism. There were many battles fought between those loyal to the Pope, and those loyal to the English crown.

As time passed, the Puritans enjoyed their progress by persecuting anyone (including other Christians) who did not pledge loyalty to their version of "the true church". By the time leading up to the American Revolution, the Puritans had butchered their way into the thirteen colonies leaving countless maimed and dead bodies in their wake.

These Puritans were a very harsh people. Methods of persecution under their authority included public humiliation (in various forms), hanging by the neck, burning at the stake, hefty monetary fines, imprisonment, and selling the absent devotee into slavery. They would cut out pieces of a person's tongue if they were found speaking against established doctrine. There are known cases of cutting off a person's ears for not "hearing the gospel". They would strip their woman naked and publicly beat and whip them bloody for talking back to their husbands. Above all, they were loyal to the crown dating back 250 years despite who was currently sitting on the throne. They were holding onto a belief established long before Charles II, George II, or George III had ever assumed power.

> What these various groups (Quakers and Anabaptists) had in common was a firm belief that Jesus's teachings on non-resistance were to be applied exactly as they were written. Jesus taught "Ye have heard that it hath been said, An eye for an eye and a tooth for a tooth: but I say unto you, that ye resist not evil: but whosoever shall smite thee on thy right cheek, turn to him the other also. And if any man will sue thee at the law, and take away thy coat, let him have thy cloak also. And whosoever shall compel thee to go a mile, go with him twain. Give to him that asketh thee, and from him that would borrow of thee turn not thou away."[3] They all believed that this teaching of Jesus did not merely apply to personal conflict but also applied to times of war. To these Christians, there was never an acceptable time to take the life of another human being on their part, even if the government ordered them to do it.

> When these non-resistant Christians finally settled in the Thirteen Colonies, they lived in Pennsylvania. At a time when most of the Colonies followed the European pattern

of having a state church, Pennsylvania was among those who did not officially have a state church, but allowed for a little more religious freedom than their Protestant neighbors in other Colonies.

King George III had allowed the Pennsylvania colony to continue as it was, just as Charles II had before him. So, these persecuted Christians were able to find a safe refuge from all of the European nations that had persecuted them since their founding. For once they had a land in which they could express their religious beliefs without fear of being hunted and/or executed by the government in the brutal fashion that they had been in Europe. The government of Pennsylvania itself was run by non-resistant Quakers, which helped the settlers to even more appreciate the freedoms they enjoyed. All of this, however, was going to change almost overnight.

While political squabbles between the non-resistant Quakers and the Protestants who were not opposed to war raged over the years prior to the American Revolution, each side maintained its particular religious beliefs, even if no compromise between the two sides was reached.[15] Even if they did not agree with each other, they maintained enough civility not to go to war prior to the American Revolution. However, with the outbreak of the War, a political shift occurred in the government of Pennsylvania. A new revolutionary government composed of various types of Protestants rapidly took over Pennsylvania and established a host of new wartime laws which put all of the conscientious objectors in a very trying position, as it would be a fiery test for all of their dearly held religious convictions.[6]

Notice how the infighting among Christians was never a cause for independence from Britain. Notice also, that the conscientious objectors (pacifist Christians) such as the Anabaptists and Quakers were permitted by the kings of England to continue practicing their religion in solidarity *without* persecution. In fact, these English kings were primarily responsible for the allowance of their peaceful practice in Pennsylvania. Whether at home or abroad, the current king of England during the American Revolution (George III) was *not* responsible for the religious disputes taking place in the colonies. So, who amongst this generation were the true tyrants?

The religious persecution of our American ancestors belongs solely to the rivaling sects of Puritans, Protestants, and Deists who had settled in the American colonies, who had then desired independence from the crown.

Religious persecution was *not* the *cause* of the American Revolution. Persecution was a byproduct of the colonial settler's unwillingness to follow Christ's teachings of peace, forgiveness, and repentance.

It was not until *money* came into the picture that the "founding fathers" decided to call colonial Christians to arms – including Quakers and Anabaptists. It was the colonial "Christian" settlers bickering about *money* and *taxes* that finally spawned the infamous revolt.

> In the eighteenth century, the American colonies became fed up with Great Britain's desire to enforce payment of taxes. Protests against the taxes could take on a violent shape. As time progressed, no resolution seemed to be in sight. The horrible chain of events ultimately culminated in America declaring its independence from Great Britain on July 4, 1776. The cause given in the Declaration

of Independence for why they felt it necessary to separate from Britain and form their own government is telling.[6]

> ... ever since King Charles II had been on the British throne, these Christians had enjoyed freedom from European persecution, and, as noted by Bercot, had no reason to take up arms against a government that had done them no wrong whatsoever[18]. Even though it had not been completely without conflict, they did not have to face execution for their religious beliefs. They always knew, though, that one day their resolute convictions would be put to the test in an outbreak of war. *"As the flames of war mount higher and higher, no man can tell whether the Cross and persecution of the defenseless Christians will not soon come, and it is, therefore, of supreme importance to prepare ourselves for such circumstances with patience and resignation, and to use all available means that can encourage steadfastness and strengthen faith."*19 Already they had willingly suffered the loss of all things when necessary during the French and Indian War (Seven Years' War) two decades earlier. These committed Christians were going to follow Jesus as they understood what that meant even if that meant paying the ultimate price. Their convictions were not just ideals to talk about during times of peace, but to be followed in any and all circumstances no matter what.[7] (emphasis mine)

The historical record proves this to be true. It was not George III who sought to diminish religious freedom in the American colonies. George III was the only reason the peaceful Quakers and Anabaptists were able to continue their settlement in Pennsylvania. It was the colonial settlers themselves who were butchering one another in the name of "true Christian Doctrine" and "freedom" from taxation.

Conquering the new world in the name of "peace" and "liberty" while persecuting anyone who disagrees with you... does any of this sound like the cornerstone of a Christian government to you?

It can be easily proven that "freedom of religion" and true Christian doctrine had *nothing* to do with the true reason for independence from Great Britain. Likewise, we can prove religious persecution was not the result of a tyrannical religious fanatic in King George III but was instead a grassroots byproduct of seeking independence from the crown.

We need to put aside this false notion that seeking religious freedom was in any way the cause of the American Revolution. It was not. Despite how brutal some of these so-called "Christians" were, the people in the American colonies were already free to practice religion as they saw fit.

Money was the sole factor driving the revolt and it is very important for every American Christian to understand how this situation developed.

~

Let us back up for a moment. Forget everything you have read up to this point. Let us now assume religious persecution was the one and only cause of the American Revolution. Let us pretend Christians were fed up with being bullied by the king of England and they had now decided to form a government founded upon religious freedom. As uncomfortable as it will be to hear this biblical reality, it must be understood and accepted for what it is.

A Christian is not permitted to take revenge against those who would persecute them for their faith. This is not to say we cannot practice self-defense against a rabid dog, but it is to say we cannot take it upon ourselves to overthrow

Christian Political Correctness

an earthly government, an earthly king, or kill our fellow Christians in the name of "freedom" and "liberty" the way our founding "fathers" deemed acceptable.

All throughout history people who remain loyal to the *right*eousness of God have been persecuted for preaching peace and repentance in the face of death and warfare.

Hear this truth!

> Then the officials said to the king, "Please have this man put to death, since he is discouraging the men of war who are left in this city and all the people, by speaking words like these to them; for this man is not seeking the well-being of this people, but rather their harm." (Jeremiah 38:4; NAS)

Jeremiah knew the sins of the nation were great. He knew God was soon to send his judgment in the form of Babylonian forces to "utterly destroy" the city of Jerusalem. Wanting to spare the lives of the soldiers, Jeremiah asked Judah to accept God's judgment and peacefully surrender. They did not, and as a result, they died in their sins.

Before the destruction of Jerusalem would take place, they sought to kill Jeremiah for wanting to make peace with the Babylonian forces marching on the city. They wanted to kill Jeremiah for preaching peace and repentance. This is *exactly* how the founding fathers treated the Quakers and Anabaptists during the American Revolution. The peace-loving Christians in Pennsylvania were already free and only wanted peace.

This does not mean all people who cling to righteousness have seen the iron hand of persecution. Many have enjoyed times of great peace and prosperity. This is a gift from God (Ecclesiastes 3:13) and it should not be taken for granted.

However, just like the *righ*teous in the Old Testament were killed for speaking truth (1 Kings 18; 19; Jeremiah 2:3; 38:4; Nehemiah 9:26; Matthew 23:35), we too may face difficult times. Just like the apostles and disciples of Christ were persecuted for speaking truth (Acts 6; 7; 9; 12; 20; 21; Revelation 6:9-11) we too may face persecution for our faith. And, just like the Quakers and the Anabaptists were martyred by other "Christian" settlers, we too may very well face deadly persecution in our beloved United States of America.

If we Americans are martyred for our religious beliefs, it will have been for all the same reasons. Because we shun war in the name of Christ, and we refuse to go to war in the name of God. Just like Jeremiah, promoting peace in the face of war is the exact reason why the Quakers and Anabaptists' faith was tested. Their patriotic "Christian" neighbors were forcing them to take up the sword to defend the colonies or die.

The issue is now presented to *you*. Will you take up the sword to save this land? Or will you trust in God, no matter what happens, to save your soul?

During the time of our trials, we are called by God to remain faithful and even to rejoice in our tribulation knowing our reward is eternal life in paradise. A life without pain, hunger, or sorrow of any kind. We must promote peace, love, hope, and charity in our lives even to those who would persecute us. And lest we forget, we are called to repentance. Never are we called to war in the name of Christ.

~

To prove the doctrine for promoting peace and repentance is true, and according to the gospel of our Lord and

Savior Jesus Christ, we will now search the bible citing all available evidence.

> When thou art in tribulation, and all these things are come upon thee, *even in the latter days*, if thou turn to the LORD thy God, and shalt be obedient unto his voice; 31(For the LORD thy God is a merciful God;) he will not forsake thee, neither destroy thee, nor forget the covenant of thy fathers which he sware unto them. (Deuteronomy 4:30-31)

From a time as long ago as when the book of Deuteronomy would have been written, this was already an established truth. The *right*eousness of God has never changed. The Israelites were told that they *would* face tribulation, and in that tribulation, they were to trust in God alone. Even in "the latter days", it says, if they are obedient to his voice, they will not be forgotten.

Allow that to sink in, if you will. Meditate on that thought. If the physical tribes of Israel are not to be forgotten, what would become of the spiritual tribes of Israel who are redeemed in Christ Jesus? Are the prophecies of Christ and his heavenly Father not intact?

> "And the LORD thy God will put all these curses upon thine enemies, and on them that hate thee, which persecuted thee." (Deuteronomy 30:7)

We are called to remain meek with a heart of forgiveness and repentance. The fate of those who do not repent of their blood-thirsty appetites has been made known to us. Theirs is a fate far worse than any persecution we face in this temporal existence. Vengeance belongs to God, not to

> O LORD my God, in thee do I put my trust: save me from all them that persecute me, and deliver me: 2Lest he tear my soul like a lion, rending it in pieces, while there is none to deliver. 3O LORD my God, if I have done this; if there be iniquity in my hands; 4If I have rewarded evil unto him that was at peace with me; (yea, I have delivered him that without cause is mine enemy:) 5Let the enemy persecute my soul, and take it; yea, let him tread down my life upon the earth, and lay mine honour in the dust. Selah. (Psalm 7:1-5)

us. Which is exactly why Jesus asks us to pray for our persecutors (Matthew 5).

This Psalm is quite revealing. It tells us a great deal about David's thought process regarding his persecutors as well as the perspective of his own sin.

First, he places his future victory firmly in the hands of God. His trust is not in his own strength or knowledge of war but in God's promises.

Second, he begs God for forgiveness. He prayed that if the current calamities he was facing were a result of something he did, he is now actively repenting.

Third, he accepts God's judgment one way or the other. He admits that if this persecution was his fault, he is ready to accept the punishment. "Let the enemy persecute my soul, and take it; yea, let him tread down my life upon the earth". David was willing to surrender his life to his persecutors in order that his sins may be forgiven. Now **that** is faith and repentance!

There is no wonder why God said of David that he was "a man after my own heart" (1 Samuel 13:14). He was willing to humble himself before the almighty power of the living God by publicly confessing his sins in front of the entire Kingdom. Name one single patriotic American (or politician) who is willing to follow David's lead to save the kingdom... yeah, nobody.

This devout faith is witnessed all throughout the bible. Never once do the authors stray from this pattern of thinking (1 Samuel 26:24; Psalm 10:2; 31:15; 35:3; 71:11; 83:15; 109:16; 119:84-86; 161; Jeremiah 17:18; Nehemiah 9:11; Lamentations 1; 3).

> Yet ye have forsaken me, and served other gods: wherefore I will deliver you no more. 14Go and cry unto the gods which ye have chosen; let them deliver you in the time of your tribulation. 15And the children of Israel said unto the LORD, *We have sinned: do thou unto us whatsoever seemeth good unto thee;* deliver us only, we pray thee, this day. (Judges 10:13-15)

It is vital for us to confess our sins and accept whatever punishment may come our way. Praying the whole time that whatever *right*eous judgement is dealt to our nation is a result of God's will to the glory of our salvation.

> O LORD, thou knowest: remember me, and visit me, and *revenge me of my persecutors;* take me not away in thy longsuffering: know that *for thy sake I have suffered rebuke.* (Jeremiah 15:15)

Jeremiah was not shy in confessing his sins, nor the sins of Judah. He was also aware that the rebuke the people were facing was due to their own disobedience. If God's people had not turned their back on Him, He would not have been forced to turn His back on them.

Identical to kind David, Jeremiah also places the revenge against his persecutors squarely on the shoulders of God. He never once claimed to seek revenge of his own accord. And like David, Jeremiah also accepted the rebuke and persecution as an act of God. He clearly said, *"for thy sake I have suffered"*. It was for the sake of God's retribution that Jeremiah was facing persecution and Judah was facing destruction.

For this cause, we can know whether we are in God's favor (Jeremiah facing persecution by his own people [like the Quakers and Anabaptists]), or whether we are the subject of God's punishment as a result of the sins of a nation (Judah and Jerusalem destroyed by Babylonian forces [America too falling like the republic of Rome]), it was God who allowed it to happen.

This is what Christian Nationalists refuse to acknowledge. One way or another, their warrior mentality will lend their hearts to fight against God's righteous judgement and they will subsequently die in their sins.

Jeremiah was persecuted by his fellow Jews for telling the truth. For continuing in God's *right*eousness, he suffered at the hands of his persecutors. In total contrast to this, Judah was punished for distancing themselves from God's *right*eousness. In both cases, God's judgement is *right*eous. Jeremiah has now found peace in God's loving embrace on the other side of this life. The rest are now separated from God, bound in the tormenting depths of sheol until the resurrection of the dead. In every case throughout the Old Testament, this is the pattern. *Right*eousness belongs to God, and God alone. The only losers are those who oppose God's perfect judgement.

> Blessed are the peacemakers: for they shall be called the children of God. 10Blessed are they which are persecuted

for righteousness' sake: for theirs is the kingdom of heaven. 11Blessed are ye, when men shall revile you, and persecute you, and shall say all manner of evil against you falsely, for my sake. 12Rejoice, and be exceeding glad: for great is your reward in heaven: *for so persecuted they the prophets which were before you...* 43Ye have heard that it hath been said, Thou shalt love thy neighbour, and hate thine enemy. 44But I say unto you, Love your enemies, bless them that curse you, do good to them that hate you, and pray for them which despitefully use you, and persecute you; 45That ye may be the children of your Father which is in heaven: for he maketh his sun to rise on the evil and on the good, and sendeth rain on the just and on the unjust. (Matthew 5:10-12; 43-45)

Blinders have been pulled over the eyes of anyone who can read these words of Christ and still claim we must create a war against our oppressors. Why must we revolt by saying "an eye for an eye", when Christ so obviously commands us to love and pray for our enemies?

How can we not understand the fate of those who persecute us is immeasurably worse than anything we face in this life? Are the trials we face worse than the depths of hell?

Matthew chapter 10... The Christian Nationalists should open their Bibles and read this text for themselves. It is likely impossible to make known any clearer a statement than is made in Jesus' own words.

Behold, I send you forth as sheep in the midst of wolves: be ye therefore wise as serpents, and harmless as doves. 17But beware of men: for they will deliver you up to the councils, and they will scourge you in their synagogues; 18And ye shall be brought before governors and kings for my sake, for a testimony against them and the Gentiles. 19But when they deliver you up, take no thought how or what ye shall speak: for it shall be given you in that same hour what ye shall speak. 20For it is not ye that speak, but the Spirit of your Father which speaketh in you. 21And the brother shall deliver up the brother to death, and the father the child: and the children shall rise up against their parents, and cause them to be put to death. 22And ye shall be hated of all men for my name's sake: but he that endureth to the end shall be saved. *23But when they persecute you in this city, flee ye into another*: for verily I say unto you, Ye shall not have gone over the cities of Israel, till the Son of man be come. 24The disciple is not above his master, nor the servant above his lord. 25It is enough for the disciple that he be as his master, and the servant as his lord. If they have called the master of the house Beelzebub, how much more shall they call them of his household? 26*Fear them not* therefore: for there is nothing covered, that shall not be revealed; and hid, that shall not be known. 27What I tell you in darkness, that speak ye in light: and what ye hear in the ear, that preach ye upon the housetops. 28*And fear not them which kill the body, but are not able to kill the soul: but rather fear him which is able to destroy both soul and body in hell.* (Matthew 10:16-28)

Notice verse 24. The servant is not above his master. Take a few minutes to meditate on this verse. What was Jesus talking about? Who is the servant, and who is the master? What did the master do, and how did the servant respond to the master's command?

Jesus is a servant to the Father in Heaven. We are supposed to be servants to our Lord Jesus (which in turn makes us servants of the Father). Remember when Jesus was faced with sorrow and temptation the night he was arrested? Jesus

Christian Political Correctness

prayed that if there was any way "this cup" could be taken from him, to make it so. But there was not. Jesus accepted the will of the Father, to go to the cross. And so shall we accept the will of Jesus, which is from the Father. Jesus showed us how to submit to the will of our master without compromise. We in turn are to submit to the will of our Lord and do as he commands under the authority of his Father, God. We are not greater than our master Jesus, and we must do as Jesus did. We must be in thought as he was in thought. We must be in deed as he was in deed. We must be in submission as he was in submission. This is the truth of the gospel message. We are servants to our master. And our master commands that we be peaceful, loving, and faithful so that our Father in Heaven will deliver us into a new life on the other side, no matter what happens here on this side. Remember what Christ said, "My kingdom is from another place". This life is the beginning of Eternity. Death is not the end! If evil men seek to destroy us, they are only destroying themselves. If they succeed in killing us, they have only succeeded in killing themselves.

> Marvel not at this: for the hour is coming, in the which all that are in the graves shall hear his voice, 29And shall come forth; they that have done good, unto the resurrection of life; and they that have done evil, unto the resurrection of damnation. (John 5:28-29)

This is why our precious Lord Jesus asks us to pray for our persecutors. Because he knows and has seen what awaits those who fail to repent. He knows what awaits the followers of Satan. He knows what awaits those who take his Father's name in vain (using God's name for vain purposes). And because he told us, *we* now know as well. We must continue speaking the truth in a world of lies, even when it means paying the ultimate price.

> He that loveth father or mother more than me is not worthy of me: and he that loveth son or daughter more than me is not worthy of me. 38And he that taketh not his cross, and followeth after me, is not worthy of me. 39He that findeth his life shall lose it: and he that loseth his life for my sake shall find it. (Matthew 10:37-39)

The Christian Nationalist movement states the opposite. It states we must love "God and Country" above all else. It states we must retain a strengthened patriotism in our hearts if we are to survive the onslaught against our "fundament Christian principles". It states the ultimate virtue of God and family is to defend our God-given constitutional republic at all costs. Forget about the gospel of Christ. Christian Nationalism states we must defend our worldly identity as a nation. A nation that our ancestors brutally stole from the native inhabitants of this land in the name of "Manifest Destiny" or some such nonsense.

On the first page of this book, I stated plainly the following.

> Many faithful believers will claim the evidence presented in this book is antagonistic toward Christian traditions in the west, and they would be right. Nevertheless, we Christians should acknowledge these truths without compromise.

This is the antagonism of which I wrote. "Christian Nationalism" is a long-winded word deployed from the mouth of Satan. Don't be fooled into thinking that if you refuse to go to war in the name of God, you are somehow an offense to Christian values in this land or an offense to Christ himself. Such a statement would have been recounted to the Quakers and Anabaptist sects, and it is the same lie Satan is forcing on American Christians today.

If God is the reason our forefathers were "given" this land, we can be assured God is now the reason it is being taken away. If true Christianity is the reason for this nation's foundation, we can rest assured it is God who has now chosen to thrust us into captivity. It is only He who raises nations up and brings them down.

So, what do we really think is going on here? What have we Americans sacrificed for the cause of Christ's kingdom?

> Then Peter began to say unto him, Lo, we have left all, and have followed thee. 29And Jesus answered and said, Verily I say unto you, There is no man that hath left house, or brethren, or sisters, or father, or mother, or wife, or children, or lands, for my sake, and the gospel's, 30But he shall receive an hundredfold now in this time, houses, and brethren, and sisters, and mothers, and children, and lands, with persecutions; and in the world to come eternal life. 31But many that are first shall be last; and the last first. (Mark 10:28-31)

Those who are held in the highest esteem in this world will be made least in the world of tomorrow. After Christ returns to personally usher in a thousand years of peace, setting up his throne in Jerusalem, all the souls who were persecuted for righteousness' sake will be resurrected into eternal life. They will reign with Christ as kings and priests over various provinces throughout the world for one thousand years. When that time is fulfilled, a new heaven and new earth will be presented to those who knowingly and willingly chose to follow Christ. It is here in the new heaven and new earth where we will live eternal life in paradise. Just like Jesus said, those who are made last through persecution will be made first in his kingdom.

> Therefore also said the wisdom of God, I will send them prophets and apostles, and some of them they shall slay and persecute: 50That the blood of all the prophets, which was shed from the foundation of the world, *may be required of this generation*; 51From the blood of Abel unto the blood of Zacharias, which perished between the altar and the temple: *verily I say unto you, It shall be required of this generation.* (Luke 11:49-51)

It is ***not*** a terrifying thing to face persecution. The judges, priests, prophets, apostles, and all disciples faced these same troubles, but they also rejoiced in their tribulations knowing their future reward was far greater than their present trials (Matthew 5:12; Luke 6:23; Acts 5:41; 16:23-25; Romans 5:3; 8:18; 12:12; 2 Corinthians 6:10; Colossians 1:24; Philippians 4:4; 1 Peter 4:12). These people were not discouraged by the prophecies; they were glorified in God's righteous judgement! They were not sorrowful in the tribulations they faced; they were grateful to be counted worthy!

Persecution and tribulations are not to be feared, they are to be embraced with spiritual discernment. This is an acceptable teaching unto all people for the glory of God's Kingdom, with eternal life as our reward.

> Rejoice and be glad, for your reward in heaven is great; for *in this same way they persecuted the prophets who were before you.* (Matthew 5:12; NAS)

Blessed are ye, when men shall hate you, and when they shall separate you from their company, and shall reproach you, and cast out your name as evil, for the Son of man's sake. 23Rejoice ye in that day, and leap for joy: for, behold, your reward is great in heaven: for *in the like manner did their fathers unto the prophets.* (Luke 6:22-23)

Remember the word that I said unto you, The servant is not greater than his lord. If they have persecuted me, they will also persecute you; if they have *kept my saying*, they will keep yours also. 21But all these things will they do unto you for my name's sake, *because they know not him that sent me.* (John 15:20)

And they departed from the presence of the council, *rejoicing that they were counted worthy to suffer shame for his name.* (Acts 5:41)

Beloved, do not be surprised at the fiery ordeal among you, which comes upon you for your testing, as though something strange were happening to you; 13but to the degree that you share the sufferings of Christ, keep on rejoicing, so that at the revelation of His glory you may also rejoice and be overjoyed. 14If you are insulted for the name of Christ, you are blessed, because the Spirit of glory, and of God, rests upon you. 15Make sure that none of you suffers as a murderer, or thief, or evildoer, or a troublesome meddler; 16*but if anyone suffers as a Christian, he is not to be ashamed, but is to glorify God in this name.* (1 Peter 4:12-19; NAS)

Jesus prophesied on multiple occasions how his followers would be persecuted. When Jesus said "the servant is not greater than his lord", it was a direct reference to persecution as a result of "keeping his sayings". Those who do not know the Father do not know or understand "his sayings". This means they certainly won't understand repentance from sin or persecution for righteousness' sake.

The Christian Nationalist's desire is to establish a "Christian" kingdom (by any means necessary), to then live comfortably, and to reap the benefits of this temporal life. And if anyone threatens that comfortable way of life, they are willing to fight to the death to defend it. But again, we must ask, what exactly are we defending on this planet? What victory do we possess by winning the war against oppression and persecution while becoming the persecutors ourselves?

> And when he had called the people unto him with his disciples also, he said unto them, Whosoever will come after me, let him deny himself, and take up his cross, and follow me. 35For whosoever will save his life shall lose it; but whosoever shall lose his life for my sake and the gospel's, the same shall save it. 36For what shall it profit a man, if he shall gain the whole world, and lose his own soul? 37Or what shall a man give in exchange for his soul? 38Whosoever therefore shall be ashamed of me and of my words in this adulterous and sinful generation; of him also shall the Son of man be ashamed, when he cometh in the glory of his Father with the holy angels. (Mark 8:34-38)

We should never forget how our lives could pass away at any moment. We must be ready at all times to face our destiny. Death can enter us in the blink of an eye. It may come by accident while driving in a car, or random burglary, theft, or assault. It will not matter. It could show itself in the form of sickness and disease or natural disasters, we would have no idea. It could arrive by the tyranny we face from world governments or for persecution in the face of deadly religious zealots. None of this is worthy of our fear and trembling. Not a single bit. We are here in this life for a very brief moment. God offers eternal happiness if we are willing to accept His call to repentance and show love to our fellow man.

However, if we desire, God *will* leave us to our own devices and allow us to accomplish our own worldly endeavors. He will allow us to succumb to the temptations of this world the same way he allowed the Israelites to have their way (1 Samuel 8), to their own destruction. He will, if we desire, give us exactly what we ask for. The absence of His presence.

If we ignore God's call to repentance, we will be separated from His loving embrace by eventually disappearing into outer darkness. It is **He** whom we should love and fear. The desires of the flesh in this fallen world are desperately worthless.

Take courage and have faith. Jesus has already overcome the world. We should seek with all our ability to follow in his footsteps.

> These things I have spoken to you so that in Me you may have peace. In the world you have tribulation, but take courage; I have overcome the world. (John 16:33)

There are several cases in the book of Acts that offer tremendous insight into not only true Christian doctrine but in this case, how to behave in the face of persecution. It would be wise for Christians to re-read the book of Acts at least once a year to refresh their memory.

We could recall the stoning of Stephen in Acts 7:54-8:2 or Saul's conversion after persecuting the church. We could re-visit how the church would retreat from their lands to find relief from their persecutors (Acts 11:19; 13:49-52). They did not stay and fight to the death. When they were faced with persecution, they simply moved locations while the apostles continued preaching as they were commanded. There is nothing wrong with retreating from a land occupied by Satan and his bloodthirsty henchmen. Jesus did not command them to stay and fight the Satanic forces gripping the territory, but rather, he told his apostles to "shake the dust off your feet" if the people refused to accept their message (Matthew 10:14; Luke 9:5; Mark 6:11). And that is precisely what the apostles did (Acts 13:51).

> And after they had preached the gospel to that city and had made a good number of disciples, they returned to Lystra, to Iconium, and to Antioch, 22strengthening the souls of the disciples, encouraging them to continue in the faith, and saying, *"It is through many tribulations that we must enter the kingdom of God."* 23When they had appointed elders for them in every church, having prayed with fasting, they entrusted them to the Lord in whom they had believed. (Acts 14:21-23; NAS)

The gospel message has proven these truths time and time again, "It is through many tribulations that we must enter the kingdom of God." (v.22) Notice what the gospel *never* says. "It is through strength and warfare that my disciples will set up the kingdom of God on earth as a constitutional republic *of* the people, *by* the people, and *for* the people."

Our loyalty should be to God the Father and His only begotten son, Jesus Christ. A collective mob of "we the people" who from millennia past have destroyed every good thing God has given them is *not* the solution. Only a delusional person could suggest "the people" should replace God the Father as an established government.

It is clear to us that Jesus taught peace and repentance, which the Christian Nationalists reject. They have no room in their hearts for longsuffering or forbearance and therefore they deny Christ's teachings while using his name for vain endeavors.

I once asked, "if you will not listen to Jesus, perhaps you will listen to Paul"... how could anyone contest the teachings of a man who himself formerly pursued "God and Country", bloodshed, and warfare as his means of evangelism? What would the Christian Nationalists say if a man who once traveled house to house executing his religious and political opposition had told them to stop fighting and listen to Jesus?

> Who shall separate us from the love of Christ? shall tribulation, or distress, or persecution, or famine, or nakedness, or peril, or sword? 36As it is written, For thy sake *we are killed all the day long; we are accounted as sheep for the slaughter.* 37Nay, in all these things we are more than conquerors through him that loved us. 38For I am persuaded, that neither death, nor life, nor angels, nor principalities, nor powers, nor things present, nor things to come, 39Nor height, nor depth, nor any other creature, shall be able to separate us from the love of God, which is in Christ Jesus our Lord. (Romans 8:35-39)

Such a man (Paul) would have a great deal to say, as you can imagine. And so, he had written extensively on this topic.

...we celebrate in hope of the glory of God. 3And not only this, but *we also celebrate in our tribulations, knowing that tribulation brings about perseverance;* 4and perseverance, proven character; and proven character, hope; 5and hope does not disappoint, because the love of God has been poured out within our hearts through the Holy Spirit who was given to us. (Romans 5:2-5; NAS)

Bless them which persecute you: bless, and curse not. 15Rejoice with them that do rejoice, and weep with them that weep. 16Be of the same mind one toward another. Mind not high things, but condescend to men of low estate. Be not wise in your own conceits. 17*Recompense to no man evil for evil.* Provide things honest in the sight of all men. 18If it be possible, as much as lieth in you, live peaceably with all men. (Romans 12:14-18)

Romans 12:18 shown above is the verse Mr. Sasquatch threw at me to somehow prove war and retaliation are justified. Reading the entire chapter, it becomes clear Paul taught nothing of the sort. The word "bless" used in verse fourteen ("*bless* them which persecute you") is the Greek word "eulogeó" (G2127: *bless*) which means; to speak well of religiously, to celebrate with praises, to speak properly, to reason with, that which benefits the hearer, to bless the hearer with speech, and so on. This is where we get our English word "eulogy" for giving remarks at a funeral. Paul was instructing the reader to remember all the blessings in their lives, and not dwell on the evil they are facing. To speak positively about their persecutors even in the face of death. Isn't that amazing? After everything the apostles faced, they were still able to find the good in their persecutors, they were able to relate to them, attempting to reason with them by way of their convictions. Paul did not curse his persecutors nor call Christians to arms over land, territorial disputes, or power and influence. Paul knew, as should we, that our persecutors are faced with eternal damnation if they don't repent. What can we possibly do to these poor hopeless souls that they have not already done to themselves? We need to speak to them about eternal life in hopes that they too should forfeit their hearts to Jesus.

> If your enemy is hungry, give him food to eat; And if he is thirsty, give him water to drink; 22For you will heap burning coals on his head, And the LORD will reward you. (Proverbs 25:21-22; NAS)

This does not mean we are allowed to pour burning coal on our enemies' heads if they ask for a drink of water. Jesus spoke in parables. This is a metaphor for searing their conscience with the word of truth. Pouring burning coals on a person's head is a simile for introducing them to *righteous*ness. We are called to plant the seed of the gospel message. Let the Holy Spirit do His work.

By going to war with our persecutors, we are denying the will of God. We are expressing our own lusts and allegiances to a world of self-justification and self-*right*eousness. This does not benefit them, or us.

After meeting with the risen Christ, and being converted to the faith, Paul chose to love his enemies. Just as Christ commanded (Matthew 5:44).

> To this very hour we go hungry and thirsty, we are in rags, we are brutally treated, we are homeless. 12We work hard with our own hands. *When we are cursed, we bless; when we are persecuted, we endure it;* 13when we are slandered, we

answer kindly. We have become the scum of the earth, the garbage of the world—right up to this moment. (1 Corinthians 4:11-13; NIV)

During the opening statement in his second letter to the Corinthians, Paul made a remark that every Christian Nationalist on the planet has blatantly ignored.

> Praise be to the God and Father of our Lord Jesus Christ, the Father of compassion and the God of all comfort, 4who comforts us in all our troubles, so that we can comfort those in any trouble with the comfort we ourselves receive from God. 5For just as we share abundantly in the sufferings of Christ, so also our comfort abounds through Christ. 6If we are distressed, it is for your comfort and salvation; if we are comforted, it is for your comfort, *which produces in you patient endurance of the same sufferings we suffer.* 7And our hope for you is firm, *because we know that just as you share in our sufferings, so also you share in our comfort.* (2 Corinthians 1:3-7; NIV)

Does anything Paul wrote, in any of his letters, give any indication that we must never allow suffering, tribulations, or persecutions to exist? What gospel message instructs us to go to war with those who disagree with our "more perfect union"? War only produces *more* suffering, *more* hopelessness, and *much* more than would have been realized by the peace-loving Christians in the thirteen colonies.

We are called to be the hands and feet of Jesus while he is away. We are called to let our love light shine, to preach peace, and to practice repentance. The gospel message of Jesus Christ could not be clearer regarding these elements of *right*eousness.

Again, Paul reiterates this in the fourth chapter of his second letter to Corinth.

> But we have this treasure in earthen containers, so that the extraordinary greatness of the power will be of God and *not from ourselves*; 8we are afflicted in every way, but not crushed; perplexed, but not despairing; 9persecuted, but not abandoned; struck down, but not destroyed; 10always carrying around in the body the dying of Jesus, so that the life of Jesus may also be revealed in our body. 11For *we who live are constantly being handed over to death because of Jesus*, so that the life of Jesus may also be revealed in our mortal flesh. (2 Corinthians 4:9; NAS)

> Receive us; we have wronged no man, we have corrupted no man, we have defrauded no man. 3I speak not this to condemn you: for I have said before, that ye are in our hearts to die and live with you. 4Great is my boldness of speech toward you, great is my glorying of you: I am filled with comfort, I am exceeding joyful in *all our tribulation*. (2 Corinthians 7:2-4)

Later in chapter 12, Paul considers "visions and revelations" (v.1) either witnessed by himself or by one of the other apostles who relayed to him these visions.

> Because of the extraordinary greatness of the revelations, for this reason, to keep me from exalting myself, there was given to me a thorn in the flesh, a messenger of Satan to torment me—to keep me from exalting myself! (2 Corinthians 12:7; NAS)

As a result of "the abundance of the revelations" Paul was from that day coveted by a "messenger of Satan to buffet me, lest I should be exalted above measure". This new lifelong encounter with a demon would become a "thorn in the flesh" (v.7). He later wrote of this *thorn* describing it as a blessing in disguise.

> For this thing I besought the Lord thrice, that it might depart from me. 9And he said unto me, *My grace is sufficient for thee: for my strength is made perfect in weakness.* Most gladly therefore will I rather glory in my infirmities, that the power of Christ may rest upon me. 10Therefore I take pleasure in infirmities, in reproaches, in necessities, *in persecutions, in distresses for Christ's sake: for when I am weak, then am I strong.* (2 Corinthians 12:8-10)

Paul never did explain what exactly this "thorn" represented to him, but we know he accepted it as a correction in his attitude and his ministry.

Whatever issues you are facing personally, whatever trials you are going through, whatever burdensome demands the world has placed on your shoulders, whatever infirmity; reproach, necessity, or persecution in distress, whatever trials you face, dearly beloved, you are not alone. Whatever thorn exists in your flesh at this moment, it could very well be a blessing in disguise. Nobody other than our Lord can tell you what exactly that blessing may be, but you should embrace it as a persecution (whether spiritual in nature or physical in the world), go to the Lord in prayer, and ask for his guidance during your trials. This "thorn in your flesh" may turn out to be the humbling encounter you had needed all along. **Exactly** like what Paul had been through. In our weakness, He is made strong. His strength is then reciprocated back to us as a blessing. This is a promise of faith.

> "...he was caught up into paradise, and heard unspeakable words, which it is not lawful for a man to utter. 5Of such an one will I glory: yet of myself I will not glory, but in mine infirmities. 6For though I would desire to glory, I shall not be a fool; for I will say the truth: but now I forbear, lest any man should think of me above that which he seeth me to be, or that he heareth of me. (2 Corinthians 12:4-6)

During Paul's apostolic journeys he was persecuted virtually everywhere he went. Did he attempt to defend his position with the sword? No. Did he persuade others to form an army to overthrow their persecutors the way America's founding fathers had? No. Paul, and everyone else, accepted persecutions as they were instructed by Jesus. Paul mentioned the apostles were "constantly being handed over to death because of Jesus", but they were not dismayed. They rejoiced!

Remember when Stephen was stoned (Acts 7-8)? Yes, many mourned over the loss (Acts 8:2), but they also blessed the Lord knowing Stephen was found worthy to suffer for righteousness' sake. This is the promise of those who do not cower in the face of persecution. And those who create armies to kill their persecutors are *not* following the commands of Jesus, nor those of our heavenly Father. It is the fighting "Christian" armies who are the cowards for not trusting in God's everlasting judgment. As Jesus said, do not fear him who destroys the body, but fear He who can destroy both soul and body in hell (Matthew 10:28).

> *That no man should be moved by these afflictions*: for yourselves know that we are appointed thereunto. 4For verily, when we were with you, *we told you before that we should suffer tribulation*; even as it came to pass, and ye know. 5For this cause, when I could no longer forbear, I sent to know your faith, lest by some means the tempter have tempted you, and our labour be in vain. (1 Thessalonians 3:3-5)

Paul knew firsthand that everyone out on the road preaching the gospel of Christ would suffer afflictions, persecutions, tribulations, whatever you want to call it. Jesus told them in advance this would happen (Matthew 10:16). They accepted their trials willingly knowing their paradisal reward was near at hand.

No matter what trials Paul was facing, he made them known in person, and in letters. The apostles, the disciples, and the everyday believer practicing their faith. They had all received afflictions at some point, which they saw as blessings. When the people began to drift away from the faith, Paul reminded them how their afflictions are not in vain but do incur righteous rewards.

> So that we ourselves glory in you in the churches of God for your patience and faith *in all your persecutions and tribulations that ye endure*. 5Which is a manifest token of the righteous judgment of God, that ye may be counted worthy of the kingdom of God, *for which ye also suffer*: 6Seeing it *is a righteous thing with God to recompense tribulation* to them that trouble you; 7And to you who are troubled rest with us, when the Lord Jesus shall be revealed from heaven with his mighty angels, 8In flaming fire *taking vengeance on them* that know not God, and *that obey not the gospel of our Lord Jesus Christ*: 9Who shall be punished with everlasting

destruction from the presence of the Lord, and from the glory of his power. (2 Thessalonians 1:4-9)

...what persecutions I endured: but out of them all the Lord delivered me. 12Yea, and *all that will live godly in Christ Jesus shall suffer persecution.* 13But evil men and seducers shall wax worse and worse, deceiving, and being deceived. (2 Timothy 3:11-13)

What can anyone add to Paul's statement above that is not already evident? "All that live godly in Christ Jesus shall suffer persecution."

Where is the motion being raised for warfare in Paul's message? Where is his call to arms? When did the apostles tell us to protest, fight, and kill our oppressors?

I know thy works, and tribulation, and poverty, (but thou art rich) and I know the blasphemy of them which say they are Jews, and are not, but are the synagogue of Satan. 10*Fear none of those things which thou shalt suffer:* ... And I gave her space to repent of her fornication; and she repented not. 22Behold, I will cast her into a bed, and them that commit adultery with her into great tribulation, except they repent of their deeds. 23And I will kill her children with death; and *all the churches shall know that I am he which searcheth the reins and hearts: and I will give unto every one of you according to your works.* (Revelation 2:9-10; 21-23)

Then one of the elders responded, saying to me, "*These who are clothed in the white robes, who are they,* and where have they come from?" 14I said to him, "My lord, you know." And he said to me, "*These are the ones who come out of the great tribulation, and they have washed their robes and made them white in the blood of the Lamb.* (Revelation 7:13-14; NAS)

We are called to peace and repentance. We are called to life in Jesus Christ. We are called to pray and long for the will of God to be accomplished on earth as it is in heaven. When Christ returns, and the Father's will is ultimately accomplished, sin will be removed from this creation just like it was removed from heaven (Revelation 12) and the Garden of Eden (Genesis 3:21-24). But before that happens, there will be a time of trying and temptation for every soul who believes in Christ. Most of us have already seen a few of these trials in one form or another. Especially when we speak truth to lies. There will be a time when we want nothing more than to turn around and head backwards. Like the moment before inevitable pain or an event we wish would not fall upon *us*. It must be so. Like ripping the bandage off an unhealed wound, or the prick of a needle we knew was coming. Like the moment devout Christians were led to the guillotines. We will experience a brief discomfort, but the healing is on its way.

The "tribulations" mentioned so frequently by Christ and the apostles are not something that will only exist at "the end of time". These tribulations have always existed. It is the persecution of the saints combined with warfare, famine, plagues, death, and natural disasters that have existed throughout all generations since the moment Christ ascended into heaven. Anyone and everyone who speaks the truth of the gospel message and does the will of the Father is going to receive persecution on earth. Glory to God, they will later receive their great rewards in paradise.

Christ's kingdom is forever. That is what those who are persecuted throughout the bible were coveting, even in times

Christian Political Correctness

of great tribulation and gnashing afflictions. The reward for not giving up hope is an everlasting paradise where all persecutors throughout history have been eternally banished to a different realm. They will be cast into outer darkness never to return.

The reason we are told to pray for our persecutors is that we know their torments will be far worse than anything they could ever do to us. We should feel very sorry for them even up to the last moment of our death. Keep in mind, the apostle Paul was present on the day Stephen was stoned… think about that mind-bender for a moment (Acts 8:1-3). These are two perfect examples of never disregarding God's hopeful love to save **all** of His wayward children (2 Peter 3:9).

> And they stoned Stephen, calling upon God, and saying, Lord Jesus, receive my spirit. 60And he kneeled down, and cried with a loud voice, *Lord, lay not this sin to their charge.* And when he had said this, he fell asleep. (Acts 7:59-60)

> And when they were come to the place, which is called Calvary, there they crucified him, and the malefactors, one on the right hand, and the other on the left. 34Then said Jesus, *Father, forgive them; for they know not what they do.* And they parted his raiment, and cast lots. 35And the people stood beholding. And the rulers also with them derided him, saying, He saved others; let him save himself, if he be Christ the chosen one. (Luke 23:33-35)

What will *you* do when your persecutors strike? What will *you* do when you are faced with a choice? Will you save your life in fear of what lies beyond the grave? Or will you give up your life knowing God is your keeper in eternity?

Jesus Christ was raised from the dead by the power of his Father in heaven. He has shown himself alive with many infallible proofs (Acts 1:3[8]). Now we must keep the faith that Christ will do the same for us, and "if it were not so, I would have told you." (John 14:1-6) If the day comes when you are given a choice between your life on earth or your life in eternity, you must remember that God will avenge your passing and you will be given a life more abundant than anything you could have ever imagined.

~

The sad and yet glorifying reality is that persecution for faith in Christ happens every single day, all around the world. America has experienced a prolonged recess from this tribulation due to the general population being predominantly Christian in their religious practices. The lack of direct deadly persecution has nothing to do with the law of the land, but everything to do with the people who occupy the land. If we begin to treat our fellow religious believers the way the founding fathers treated those who would not "man up" or "get out of the way", we will have begun this deadly persecution once again. Exactly like the American Revolution. The only difference is that we now have a vast population of non-Christians growing in this land. They will most likely not hesitate to join the cause in offending peaceful Christians.

We are facing perilous times in America, but this is not a reason to lose hope! By all means, the opposite is true! We have every reason to rejoice!

"Blessed are those who are persecuted for righteousness sake, theres is the kingdom of Heaven!"

Christian Political Correctness

We will now end this segment with the parable of the sower and the seed. (Matthew 13:1-23; Mark 4:1-20; Luke 8:4-15)

...Behold, a sower went forth to sow; 4And when he sowed, some seeds fell by the way side, and the fowls came and devoured them up: 5Some fell upon stony places, where they had not much earth: and forthwith they sprung up, because they had no deepness of earth: 6And when the sun was up, they were scorched; and because they had no root, they withered away. 7And some fell among thorns; and the thorns sprung up, and choked them: 8But other fell into good ground, and brought forth fruit, some an hundredfold, some sixtyfold, some thirtyfold. 9Who hath ears to hear, let him hear. (Matthew 13:3-9)

"Listen then to the parable of the sower. 19When anyone hears the word of the kingdom and does not understand it, the evil one comes and snatches away what has been sown in his heart. This is the one sown with seed beside the road. 20The one sown with seed on the rocky places, this is the one who hears the word and immediately receives it with joy; 21yet he has no firm root in himself, but is only temporary, and *when affliction or persecution occurs because of the word, immediately he falls away.* 22And the one sown with seed among the thorns, this is the one who hears the word, and the anxiety of the world and the deceitfulness of wealth choke the word, and it becomes unfruitful. 23But the one sown with seed on the good soil, this is the one who hears the word and understands it, who indeed bears fruit and produces, some a hundred, some sixty, and some thirty times as much." (Matthew 13:18-23; NAS)

This is not only a parable about spreading the gospel message, but a prophecy regarding persecution. Christ foretold there would be people who accept the word of God gladly, but when they are faced with persecution for Christ's name, they cannot endure it. They have no strength in their convictions. They are plants without roots. They have fallen away from the true gospel message.

Is any of this starting to sound familiar?

CHAPTER 3

PAYING TAXES TO CAESAR

"No man can serve two masters: for either he will hate the one, and love the other; or else he will hold to the one, and despise the other. Ye cannot serve God and mammon." (Mathew 6:24)

What is more inevitable or even more predictable than the concept of people fighting over money? If the god you serve requires you to elevate the value of money and personal interest above our supernatural calling to assist in the wellbeing of others (service), then there is nothing more predictable nor inevitable in all the world. Money is the root of all evil.

Jesus Christ never commanded his followers to fight and kill each other to resolve their financial hardships. This fact should be evident to all bible believing Christians, but it is not. We are now faced with a dire need to recite the obvious. What were Jesus' commandments regarding money and taxes?

Before revealing the simplest answers belonging to this forgotten gospel, we need to first address the imposed monetary policies set in place at the time leading up to the American Revolution. Understanding the forces and restrictions on currencies used at that time is fundamental when trying to comprehend the actions of our founding fathers.

Money is likely the single most important motivating factor when attempting to assemble a group of people to action *if* it is implemented well. The same is true for the opposite. When strict monetary policies negatively impact honest hard-working people, a revolution against the people's government is bound to ensue. Time and time again this is the case. And it was certainly the case once again with Great Britain and her wayward thirteen colonies.

When it came to matters of faith, George III (king of England 1760-1820) did *not* persecute his Christian subjects, nor was religious persecution authorized by his royal signature. However, no earthly king in their right mind would allow the money coffers to dry up on *their* watch. The religious faith of a king's subjects is one thing, but the king's ability to regulate currency in his kingdom is another thing altogether. To this degree, George III was every bit as cunning a King as he *needed* to be. Not because he was a Tyrant, as our founding fathers made accusations, but because he inherited one hell of a mess, and his hand was *forced* to do *something* about it. The British crown was facing troubles in America long before George III was born.

~

The Currency Act of 1751 was the first of two major financial declarations penned by the King of England (in this case, George II – predecessor and kin to George III). The intention was to regain control of the exchange of currencies in the thirteen colonies as well as a direct attempt to curb inflation.

After the French and Indian wars, the value of the banknotes printed in the colonies had been substantially depreciated. This was caused by the overprinting of colonial banknotes not backed by hard assets. When crossing paths with the British Pound Sterling, which was backed by precious metals, the English merchants began losing money from trading goods using these devaluing colonial currencies.

In the decades leading up to the American Revolution, there were essentially three major forms of currency being used in the colonies. Locally produced goods and services (a.k.a., bartering) could be used as opposed to "money" in the sense modern societies are accustomed. Anybody in possession of land, a product, a service, or a trade of any kind could essentially make a living without paper money. It was as simple as that. If you were smart enough and capable enough to work for your food, you would always have food on the table.

Even with bartering in full swing as an acceptable means for trade, the colonies were not opposed to using "banknotes". If the note was backed by the value of the land owned by the individual, it was as good as gold or silver. Landowners were allowed to produce banknotes against their property through the colonial banks.

The third major currency on the table at that time was of course hard assets. Gold, silver, and other precious valuables. All the above were traded commodities in the economic practices of the British American colonies.

As time passed, and after the debilitating economic events surrounding the French and Indian wars, the settlers were faced with paying off debts to their foreign and domestic counterparts who helped finance the war. These so-called "bills of credit" were nothing more than an "I owe you" which were essentially worthless to the British merchants once the merchants were back on British soil. The inflation caused by these actions had not gone unnoticed back in London.

At the direction of the king, George II (grandfather of George III), and his prime minister on whom he relied heavily, the declaration was made. The Currency Act of 1751 can be summed up as; 1) no new public banks were allowed to be created anywhere in the colonies, 2) the existing banks were no longer allowed to print *new* paper money, and 3) the colonies could use their "bills of credit" to furnish public debt (such as taxes owed to the crown), but they were prohibited from using their banknotes for private debt (such as payments to sea merchants). When dealing with merchant ships, the colonies were now forced to pay with hard assets. Whatever paper money was circulating in the colonies at that time was to be the last allotment for public debt, and never again to be used for private debt.

Although short-sighted, this was a smart move by the king as it prevented any further inflation that would arise from the colonies' overprinting. This royal decree also prevented the merchants from losing money on their trade deals with the colonial settlers by not allowing the settlers to pay their debts in colonial banknotes.

The colonies now had to pay merchants exclusively in hard assets which further exacerbated their financial situation over time. The colonial money system was seeing signs of instability while the British Pound was securely backed by the king's royal chest. The crown must have believed this would somehow fix the issues they were seeing in the colonies. It was a one-sided win-win for the king of England.

George II was never a fan of kingdom politics as is noted by several historians. He trusted his prime ministers and parliament to handle the affairs of the state without too much interference. Although, the king did ultimately approve and sign this decree. Unbeknownst to anyone at the time, kicking a man while he is down is not a good idea. Especially not when that man is your kinfolk holding the keys to the new world... a world 3500 miles across a treacherous ocean.

As you can imagine, many high-browed financially backed politicians in the colonies were not happy with the King's Currency Act.

~

Years later, a bashful and inexperienced young man would be thrust into power when his grandfather (George II) died unexpectedly. George III assumed the throne in 1760 at the ripe age of twenty-two, inheriting a disaster not of his own making. It is said he was a man of faith in his own right but even men of faith have a job to do. One of those jobs was the Currency Act of 1764 decreed and signed by his own pen.

The former restriction put in place prohibiting the printing of new paper bills had been lifted. The colonies could now open new banks and print new bills... with one stipulation. The new bills could not be used to pay their debts to Britain. In the Currency Act signed by his granddad, colonial banknotes were acceptable for paying taxes (public debt) but not merchandise (private debt). In the new decree signed by George III, the colonies were now forbidden from using banknotes for any reason other than their own localized colonial currency.

> Parliament had always envisioned that its American colonies should use a monetary system similar, if not identical, to the British system of "hard currency" based on the pound sterling. Feeling that it would be too hard for it to

regulate colonial paper money, Parliament chose to simply declare it worthless instead.

The colonies felt devastated by this and protested angrily against the act. Already suffering a deep trade deficit with Great Britain, colonial merchants feared the lack of their own hard capital would make the situation even more desperate.

The Currency Act exacerbated tensions between the colonies and Great Britain and is considered to be one of the many grievances that led to the American Revolution and the Declaration of Independence.[9]

As Benjamin Franklin would later say, it was not only *"one of many* grievances that led to the American Revolution", but it was in fact the single greatest factor. As it always is, ***money*** was the reason to revolt.

WHEREAS great quantities of paper bills of credit have been created and issued in his Majesty's colonies or plantations in America, by virtue of acts, orders, resolutions, or votes of assembly, making and declaring such bills of credit to be legal tender in payment of money: and whereas such bills of credit have greatly depreciated in their value, by means whereof debts have been discharged with a much less value than was contracted for, to the great discouragement and prejudice of the trade and commerce of his Majesty's subjects, by occasioning confusion in dealings, and lessening credit in the said colonies or plantations: for remedy whereof, may it please your most excellent Majesty, that it may be enacted; and be it enacted by the King's most excellent majesty, by and with the advice and consent of the lords spiritual and temporal, and commons, in this present parliament assembled, and by the authority of the same, That from and after the first day of September, one thousand seven hundred and sixty four, no act, order, resolution, or vote of assembly, in any of his Majesty's colonies or plantations in America, shall be made, for creating or issuing any paper bills, or bills of credit of any kind or denomination whatsoever, declaring such paper bills, or bills of credit, to be legal tender in payment of any bargains, contracts, debts, dues, or demands whatsoever; and every clause or provision which shall hereafter be inserted in any act, order, resolution, or vote of assembly, contrary to this act, shall be null and void. (Excerpt from the Currency Act of 1764)

In summary, the over-printing of colonial banknotes to pay off foreign debts led to the inflation of colonial currencies. This inflation then led to English merchants not getting paid in full due to the devaluing of said currency. Angry merchants and unpaid taxes led to two different Currency Acts signed by the King(s) of England. Subsequently, it was these Currency Acts that led to the American Revolution.

It is evident then to suggest the hardships leading up to the American Revolution were not exclusively caused by a "Tyrant" king, but were a great deal, at least in part, self-inflicted wounds by the colonialist leadership themselves. If the colonial bankers had not overinflated their own banknotes, there would have been no cause for the Currency Acts of George II, and later George III. And therefore, if there were no Currency Acts regulating the colonies as a result of inflation, there would have been no American Revolution.

The foundation of America had nothing whatsoever to do with "fundamental Christian principles" as we have all been led to believe. It was all about currency exchange and monetary policy. The evidence would suggest we modern Christians have been fooled into believing a false characterization of our founding fathers. That, or it is a much more elaborate religious hoax to rewrite history for the purpose of persuading Christians to join the fight for "the homeland". Satan, once again, has been deceiving the masses all the while using the name of Christ and "God" to accomplish *his* will.

We can now answer this question with confidence. Why did our founding fathers declare war for independence from Great Britain? Because a wise few at the top had indebted the colonial settlers to their earthly king by way of usury.

~

While continuing the endeavor I had sought in this chapter's original outline, I had found myself so deep down the proverbial rabbit hole I could no longer see the light. I have chosen to *not* disclose my findings but only to continue in the direction I had originally intended… proving the gospel message of peace and repentance to be true.

A journey into the subterranean chambers mentioned above would require the efforts of an entirely new book, or series of books, devoted specifically to that subject. While this is possible, it will not be done here, nor in any future publication by my hand. As the saying goes, sometimes the truth is stranger than fiction. Instead, I will offer one quote from Benjamin Franklin and one quote from our Lord and Savior Jesus Christ. The rest will be left to the readers' own divination.

> "The refusal of King George to allow the colonies to operate an honest money system, which freed the ordinary man

from clutches of the money manipulators was probably the prime cause of the revolution." – Benjamin Franklin

A more concise and direct statement could not have been made. It is often said *a picture is worth a thousand words*, but a quote of this nature is worth even more. It is odd to think Mr. Franklin saw the overprinting of his own colonial banknotes as "an honest money system", but that is indeed what he claimed.

It is well known Mr. Franklin was instrumental as one of the few writers to initially draft the *Declaration of Independence*, as well as many other defining moments leading up to and proceeding with the American Revolution. For a man of his stature and influence to make a statement about the "prime cause" of the revolution is striking, to say the least. It was all about money. Money is what drove our founding fathers to kill their peaceful Christian brothers for the sake of their own "liberty", "freedom", and "a more perfect union".

Now behold, our Lord Jesus Christ.

> Then the Pharisees went and plotted together how they might trap Him in what He said. 16And they sent their disciples to Him, along with the Herodians, saying, "Teacher, we know that You are truthful and teach the way of God in truth, and do not care what anyone thinks; for You are not partial to anyone. 17Tell us then, what do You think? Is it permissible to pay a poll-tax to Caesar, or not?" 18But Jesus perceived their malice, and said, "Why are you testing Me, you hypocrites? 19Show Me the coin used for the poll-tax." And they brought Him a denarius. 20And He said to them, "Whose image and inscription is this?" 21They said to Him, "Caesar's." Then He said to them, "Then pay to Caesar the things that are Caesar's; and to

God the things that are God's." 22And hearing this, they were amazed; and they left Him and went away. (Matthew 22:15-22; NAS)

The word "poll-tax" used in this verse (G2778; *kensos*) is of Latin origin, referring to the census tax required of all non-Roman citizens residing within a Roman province. This tax was to be collected along with census data in whatever territory the person would reside. Because this was Roman law, and Jews were not considered Roman citizens, they were taxed by Rome.

The religious leaders in Judea tried, once again, to trap Jesus in his own words. They hoped in vain that if they could somehow persuade Jesus to publicly denounce the census tax to Caesar, they could report this tax violation to the local publican and Jesus would be arrested and tried. Problem solved.

What was Jesus' response? He essentially told them to stop complaining and pay their taxes to Rome… he then reminded them to give to God what belongs to God. What Jesus did *not* say is, "rebel… form a government of your own inclination and kill anyone who disagrees with you." That much should be obvious, but it is clearly *not* obvious to the Christian Nationalists. Nor was it obvious to our "Christian" founding fathers. They went to war – the war for independence – and killed anyone who got in their way. Including peaceful non-resistant Christians.

Think for yourself, dear reader, does any of this sound like the actions of a Christian disciple to you? Do these actions in any way resemble the foundation of a "Christian nation"? How exactly was this nation built on "fundamental Christian principles"? They printed their way into debt, then went to war to get out from under that debt, killing and

Christian Political Correctness

maiming anyone who stood in opposition. How in God's holy name can anyone claim these actions resemble the "first precepts of Christianity"?

Even if the founders did identify as "Christian", that does not prove they were following Christ's commandments any more than calling myself a duck makes me a duck. Think about it. If I call myself a duck, does that mean I am a duck? No, it means I am mentally ill. And if I call myself a "Christian" while committing religious genocide against others who don't agree with my "true doctrine" or my monetary policies, it does now make me a Christian. It makes me a murderer, and I need to repent immediately!

The founding fathers of the United States of America could not pay their taxes with over-inflated currencies. They went to war to protect their colonies from excess hyperinflation (caused by their own overprinting of colonial banknotes) and the subsequent Currency Acts that followed. Even if the entire event was forced by proxy from an outside influence, we are still faced with an irrelevant paradox of "why".

Jesus, in his perfect knowledge of *right*eousness, told the people to stop complaining about paying taxes to Caesar and start focusing on God, and what God desires.

Taxes have existed all throughout history. Every civilization to have ever existed has issued taxes, some harsher than others. Including the United States of America.

As an IT guy, I made about $67,000 this past year. After taxes, I brought home about $44,000. I then had to pay taxes on all goods and services I purchased with the already taxed money. After I purchased the taxed items, with taxed money, I then had to pay taxes on what I already own, such as my house and my car. Then, if I fail to pay the taxes in the coming years, I will be penalized (another form of tax). After sitting down and doing the math, I had roughly $30,000 remaining from the original $67,000 as disposable income (give or take a couple thousand for the territorial cost of living). This means the government took approximately 60% of my money in taxes. About half of that went to paying my family's bills and other societal decrees. What remained was about $15,000 of the original $67,000. That is a *lot* of taxes.

Now... does that give me the right to form a militia, overthrow my government (war), "reclaim the republic", and institute a new government with me and my warmonger buddies at the helm? Well, yes. According to the Constitution of the United States of America (the Second Amendment), that is exactly what it means.

The point is, according to the teachings of Christ, it does not. It is never acceptable to cause war for the sake of making our lives "more perfect", as our founding fathers once wrote.

Who the hell do we think we are to suggest killing people to pay fewer taxes or fix our self-inflicted money problems, is acceptable to God?

The idea of men in power forcing their subject populations to pay taxes has never changed. Not anywhere throughout the history of the world. The only thing that *has* changed is our relationship with those who would be our masters. Did you know Jesus and his apostles told us to obey our masters as slaves?

Will we allow God to take vengeance in His time, or will we take it upon ourselves to kill our oppressors to form "a more perfect union"?

Nations and territories will come and go, the USA is no exception. The good news is, the word of God will live forever! *You* will live forever, dear reader, *if* you obey the word of God.

It is Christ whom we should follow and mimic in our daily lives. We should seek the Father's *right*eousness, and not the earthly lusts that we consider *right* in our own eyes.

If we seek, as our founding fathers sought, to adhere to our own self-*right*eous interests and ideologies, then we are denying the will of our Father in heaven. It truly is this simple. If we love money so much that we are willing to kill to get what we want, then we may very well succeed in building our very own earthly kingdom. But we will ***never*** be granted entrance into the kingdom of God.

> No one can serve two masters. Either you will hate the one and love the other, or you will be devoted to the one and despise the other. You cannot serve both God and money. (Matthew 6:24; NIV)

The passage shown above is a direct quote from Jesus. Let that sink in…

Ask yourself in all sincerity, after reading the gospel of our Lord and Savior Jesus Christ, what type of Christian would behave as the founding fathers behaved? What type of Christian is willing to kill to pay fewer taxes or to stop the hyperinflation of a currency? The answer is of course a "Christian Nationalist" or a Christian Deist. They are still to this day willing to commit murder for the benefit of the republic. Christian Nationalists refuse to admit it, but none of them are willing to follow Christ's commandments. They are in fact following a Christ of their own design.

When approached with this evidence, they remain willingly ignorant lashing out at anyone who opposes them, just like their founding fathers. We can be assured that among them there has risen a sect who are only "playing the part". They are liars and deceivers, wolves in sheep's clothing"

(Matthew 7:15), using Christ's name to kill for the sake of "God and Country".

Just like in the days of the initial *Declaration of Independence*, they tug at our heartstrings, our fears, and our passions, with the hope that *we* will once again join their battle for a new revolution.

May God have mercy on their souls for what they are doing, and may God have mercy on us all for allowing this heresy to invade our Christian churches. Christianity should unite with this message preaching peace and repentance, for the kingdom of God is a hand.

~

I cannot speak for the founding fathers, and I will not speak for Jesus Christ. I am not as educated, traveled, or influential as those men were, and I am *nothing* compared to Christ. However, I can now speak on my own behalf.

I don't like paying taxes any more than the next non-citizen of Rome, but I am not going to kill people with the hope that someone, somewhere, will eventually lower my taxes.

I don't like hyperinflation taking place in modern America (the same way it was taking place during the American Revolution), but I am not going to kill people with the hope that someone somewhere will help bring the currency back to some vague "great again" standard.

I don't like the Zionists big banks running the global economy, but I am not going to sacrifice my soul for the sole purpose of "liberty" and "freedom" from their tyrannical grip on planet Earth. I don't care if they rule the world, and neither should you. Our treasures reside in the new heaven and new earth.

But according to His promise we are looking for new heavens and a new earth, in which righteousness dwells. (2 Peter 3:13; NAS)

Slaves, be obedient to those who are your masters according to the flesh, with fear and trembling, in the sincerity of your heart, as to Christ; 6not by way of eye-service, as people-pleasers, but as slaves of Christ, doing the will of God from the heart. 7With goodwill render service, as to the Lord, and not to people, 8knowing that whatever good thing each one does, he will receive this back from the Lord, whether slave or free. And masters, do the same things to them, and give up threatening, knowing that both their Master and yours is in heaven, and there is no partiality with Him. (Ephesians 6:5-9; NAS)

Servants, be subject to your masters with all respect, not only to those who are good and gentle, but also to those who are harsh. 19For this finds favor, if for the sake of conscience toward God a person endures grief when suffering unjustly. (1 Peter 2:18-19; NAS)

Urge slaves to be subject to their own masters in everything, to *be pleasing, not argumentative,* 10not stealing, but showing all good faith so that they will adorn the doctrine of God our Savior in every respect. (Titus 2:9; NAS)

From the time of the ancient Egyptians, until the time of Christ in Rome (Jerusalem)… from the time of Christ, until the United States of America… the monetary policies as well as the means for trade and commerce have fluctuated continuously with no stabilization of any kind. It will ***always*** be this way. Satan is angry with the inhabitants of earth because he knows his time is short (Revelation 12:12). We have nothing to fear because we know this life is not the end. Satan has everything to fear because he has already made his decision to go to war with God. He does everything he can to kill those who follow God's commandments (Revelation 13:7). The life we are living is a very brief and very fleeting existence compared to eternity (1 Corinthians 2:9). What exactly are the Christian Nationalists fighting for? More money? Fewer taxes? The end to government tyranny? None of this is relevant in the eye of eternity, nor will it ever be possible until Christ comes back to fix it himself, as promised. None of this will ever be accomplished until Satan is taken out of the way after all things have been fulfilled. Read Revelation 19 through 22. We should be spiritually preparing for the promise of Christ's inevitable return, and our inevitable physical resurrection from the earthly grave, not physically fighting for a "more perfect" set of conditions in this temporal existence.

As Christ commanded, give to Caesar what belongs to Caesar (a self-proclaimed god on planet Earth who will one day be cast into outer darkness), but give to God what belongs to God… you. You belong to God. Give Him your heart. Give Him your perseverance. Give God your faith and receive your heavenly rewards.

CHAPTER 4

The Founding Fathers

"And do not call anyone on earth your father; for only One is your Father, He who is in heaven." (Matthew 23:9; NAS)

People tend to throw the word around very loosely. "Christian". Knowing the history of the church dating back to the times of the apostles, and how the church has fractured into so many different sects, it *should* be no surprise to learn the American architects did not see eye to eye regarding religious matters. It may even come as a shock to learn a good portion of the founders were not practicing Christians at all.

Several of these men ascribed only to deism. They believed in "God", based on the rational thoughts of man, or "reason", as well as the physical evidence presented in creation supporting intelligent design. They also believed God (whoever God is) would have no direct interaction with mankind on His own divine accord. Therefore, the deists collectively believe Jesus and his pacifist attitude toward tyrants is not to be trusted. To the deist, Jesus is *not* an authority from God.

It is a little-known fact that the people who drafted the Constitution of the United States of America were deists. Since this is in fact the truth, why do the TV and radio pulpiteers patently state the opposite when addressing their Christian financial supporters?

> Drawing from the scientific and philosophical work of such figures as Jean-Jacques Rousseau, Isaac Newton, and John Locke, Deists argued that human experience and rationality—rather than religious dogma and mystery—determine the validity of human beliefs. In his widely read The Age of Reason, Thomas Paine, the principal American exponent of Deism, called Christianity "a fable." Paine, the protégé of Benjamin Franklin, denied "that the Almighty ever did communicate anything to man, by…speech,…language, or…vision." Postulating a distant deity whom he called "Nature's God" (a term also used in the Declaration of Independence), Paine declared in a "profession of faith":
>
> > "I believe in one God, and no more; and I hope for happiness beyond this life. I believe in the equality of man; and I believe that religious duties consist in doing justice, loving mercy, and in endeavoring to make our fellow-creatures happy."
>
> Thus, Deism inevitably subverted orthodox Christianity. Persons influenced by the movement had little reason to read the Bible, to pray, to attend church, or to participate in such rites as baptism, Holy Communion, and the laying on of hands (confirmation) by bishops.
>
> …Deistic thought was immensely popular in colleges from the middle of the 18th into the 19th century. Thus, it

influenced many educated (as well as uneducated) males of the Revolutionary generation. Although such men would generally continue their public affiliation with Christianity after college, they might inwardly hold unorthodox religious views. Depending on the extent to which Americans of Christian background were influenced by Deism, their religious beliefs would fall into three categories: non-Christian Deism, Christian Deism, and orthodox Christianity.[10]

Such men of deistic faith would include our beloved George Washington, Benjamin Franklin, Thomas Jefferson, and John Adams, to name a few. The names people remember most from history. The names that overshadow outspoken Christians such as Benjamin Rush. The same names so often cited by right-wing evangelical Christian radio and television. It is these men who openly denied Christ, particularly when other members of the delegation made attempts to include Christ's name in *their* new government. If the Constitution of the United States of America was at all inspired by the virtues from bible believing Christians, they will forever be overshadowed by the persuasive strength and influence of the deistic faith of our waring forefathers.

Below are a few facts likely not known by many God-fearing Christians. Feel free to research this information for yourself online, or at your local library.

We could begin with the infamous story of George Washington's cherry tree. Did Washington at the age of six receive a hatchet as a present? Did he then in fact damage his father's cherry tree with said hatched? Did he then confess to doing so at the behest of his father's anger only to say, "I cannot tell a lie, Dad. I did cut the tree with my hatched"? As the story goes, young George's dad was so thrilled with the boy's admission that he said, "George's honesty is worth more than a thousand trees."

> The guy who created the myth, Mason Locke Seems, was a Federalist admirer of order and self-discipline who wanted to present Washington as the perfect role model, especially for young Americans. When Washington died, many people wanted to know his story outside of his Revolutionary War/Presidential life. The author decided to create the myth to play into Washington's unwritten childhood and relationship with his father. He wanted to imply that Washington's public greatness was due to his private virtues. Ironically, he told lies in order to create a myth that served to illustrate the importance of telling the truth.[11]

If you spend any time researching this information, you will also find the truth. The cherry tree story is a disingenuous myth created by the Anglican pastor, author, and bookseller; Parson Weems.

As Christians, we should ask ourselves, what human is incapable of lying? What man has perfect morals? How and why did this *perfect man* become the leader of a bloody revolutionary army? And why was this odd fable told to us in our infant years at grammar school?

Years after the war, Washington's pastor in Pennsylvania would write that he never held Christian beliefs, but that he was instead heavily influenced by deism. All the while still a member of the church in Pennsylvania. There is no difference between the attitude of George Washington and the politicians of today who "play the part" for political gain with their constituents.

Some have argued Benjamin Franklin only became a Christian later in life, but by that time it was too late to undo the many years of deistic influence he forced on this new government. Historians focus more on Franklins encouraging patriotism while ignoring his cryptic statements implying regret.

"Whatever is begun in anger ends in shame."

Why would he say such a thing? And what is meant by his further remarks?

"Life's tragedy is that we get old too soon and wise too late."

To what tragedy was he referring? And why would a man who was so instrumental in forming "a more perfect union" (allegedly a Christian nation), say such things only a few years after the nation's founding? What did he know that he was not telling the rest of us?

Despite his often poetic indifference to the union he helped inspire, he would make statements that were clearly contrary to the teachings of Christ. Meaning, he was neither for the democratic republic he helped forge nor for Christian theology.

"If everyone is thinking alike, then no one is thinking."

Franklin asserts those who "think freely" would be the true benefactors of a liberated society. To a certain extent, this is true. If we blindly follow our corrupt leaders, we are not following Christ but are in fact being led down a path of self-destruction. Nonetheless, his statements are a slap in the face to Christ and the apostles. Christ taught and practiced the opposite. Christ taught we should all be of one heart, mind, and soul.

> And the multitude of them that believed were of one heart and of one soul: neither said any of them that ought of the

things which he possessed was his own; but they had all things common. 33And with great power gave the apostles witness of the resurrection of the Lord Jesus: and great grace was upon them all. (Acts 4:32-33)

Fulfil ye my joy, that ye be likeminded, having the same love, being of one accord, of one mind. 3*Let nothing be done through strife or vainglory...* (Philippians 2:2-3)

For those who are in Christ, there is a great oneness, a mutual understanding of how *love* governs all actions. Without the love of God, there will be no peace on earth. This idea could not be more remote to a deist like Benjamin Franklin.

"Make yourself sheep and the wolves will eat you."

Yes, Mr. Franklin. They will. This is why Jesus desired that we be as wise as serpents and as harmless as doves.

Behold, I send you forth as sheep in the midst of wolves: be ye therefore wise as serpents, and harmless as doves. (Matthew 10:16)

Deist teachings contradict Jesus' gospel on every front. Deists would have *us* become wolves, leaving the harmless dove mentality behind while devouring anyone or anything standing in the way of our earthly conquest. They would have us leave our good shepherd, our King, our Christ. They would have us flock to the "higher education" institutions of the day.

"Freedom is not a gift bestowed upon us by other men, but a right that belongs to us by the laws of God and nature."

They love using the phrase, "God and nature". These men worship the creation while denying their creator; Jesus

Christ (John 1). The truth is everywhere, hidden in plain sight. These men were not Christians!

"Man will ultimately be governed by God or by tyrants."

This statement is ignorant on many levels. Even with tyrants in control, we can still be governed by the laws of God the Father, and his only begotten son Jesus Christ. We do not need a representative in Congress, or the Senate to follow God's perfect law of love. Anyone who does not know this truth is admittedly not a Christian.

Tyrants have always existed. Even during the time of Rome while Christ was in his pre-resurrection flesh, the land was ruled by tyrants. Until Christ's return, the tyrants will continue to exist as our earthly overlords. Tyrants have been running the beast system of government for millennia. From ancient Egypt to Assyria, from Babylon to Meda-Persia, from Greece to Rome, to the reformation. From Great Britain to the United Nations, headquartered right here in our very own "more perfect union" in New York City.

Tyrants rule over their subject populations as slave masters. We are slaves, and they are our earthly masters. That's just the way it is, and that's okay! The tyrants may do whatsoever they please without fear of retribution in this life, but they have a judgement coming that they know nothing about. Christ and his apostles told us (the slaves) to obey our masters. To love them and treat them will all respect, whether it is earned or not.

> Servants, be obedient to them that are your masters according to the flesh, with fear and trembling, in singleness of your heart, as unto Christ; 6Not with eyeservice, as menpleasers; but as the servants of Christ, doing the will of God from the heart; 7With good will doing service, as to the Lord, and not to men: 8Knowing that whatsoever

good thing any man doeth, the same shall he receive of the Lord, whether he be bond or free. 9And, ye masters, do the same things unto them, forbearing threatening: knowing that your Master also is in heaven; neither is there respect of persons with him. (Ephesians 6: 5-9)

Servants, be subject to your masters with all respect, not only to those who are good and gentle, but also to those who are harsh. (1 Peter 2:18; NAS)

In doing so, we are ensuring our place of rulership over them in the next life.

Then Peter began to say unto him, Lo, we have left all, and have followed thee. 29And Jesus answered and said, Verily I say unto you, There is no man that hath left house, or brethren, or sisters, or father, or mother, or wife, or children, or lands, for my sake, and the gospel's, But he shall receive an hundredfold now in this time, houses, and brethren, and sisters, and mothers, and children, and lands, with persecutions; and in the world to come eternal life. 31But many that are first shall be last; and the last first. (Mark 10:30-31)

And when he had opened the fifth seal, I saw under the altar the souls of them that were slain for the word of God, and for the testimony which they held: 10And they cried with a loud voice, saying, How long, O Lord, holy and true, dost thou not judge and avenge our blood on them that dwell on the earth? 11And white robes were given unto every one of them; and it was said unto them, that they should rest yet for a little season, until their fellowservants also and their brethren, that should be killed as they were, should be fulfilled. (Revelation 6:9-11)

During the millennium reign of Christ on planet Earth, those who lost their lives to tyrants for the sake of the gospel will be appointed rulers over the peoples of the earth. Love will become the law of the land, once and for all. What a glorious day it will be.

And I saw thrones, and they sat upon them, and judgment was given unto them: and I saw the souls of them that were beheaded for the witness of Jesus, and for the word of God, and which had not worshipped the beast, neither his image, neither had received his mark upon their foreheads, or in their hands; and they lived and reigned with Christ a thousand years. (Revelation 20:4)

We in the USA are currently ruled by a tyrannical *beast* system of government. A *beast*, ironically, that was created by the waring deists we refer to as our "Christian" founding fathers.

If we focus on the commandments of Christ, none of this global tyranny can harm us. Whether inside the United States or abroad. All our worrying and strife is for naught.

And which of you by worrying can add a day to his life's span? 26Therefore if you cannot do even a very little thing, why do you worry about the other things? (Luke 12:25-26; NAS)

Whether we live in an ancient dictatorship or the modern USA, it is all the same beast system of Government that has existed for thousands of years. In the future kingdom of

God, Christ will be sitting on his throne in the New Jerusalem (Revelation 21), and the beast system of government will be dismantled worldwide from top to bottom.

If you put your faith in government officials who deny Christ, you too will have denied Christ in your heart. You will be found wanting in vain. To resolve this issue, it is as simple as getting out of line, turning around, and heading back in the other direction. Head back to the gospel message and begin again in Jesus' truth and *righ*teousness.

Benjamin Franklin had no hope in Christ, the resurrection, or the coming judgment. Which is why the Government he founded failed; it was **not** a Christ-centered government. The United States of America was not founded as a Christian nation. It was quite specifically, an anti-Christ government in its very definition. They rejected Christ in their letters (the Declaration of Independence), in their words (written letters and speeches), and in their deeds (killing their Christian constituents in the name of "liberty" and "freedom of religion").

As Benjamin Franklin stated in his own words for all the world to read, his deistic government was hopeless and despotic.

> "This [the U.S. Constitution] is likely to be administered for a course of years and then end in despotism... when the people shall become so corrupted as to need despotic government, being incapable of any other."

Alas, Mr. Franklin has told the truth. He unwittingly admitted that without Christ, our worldly efforts are in vain and doomed to failure. For all intents and purposes in this year, 2024, the Constitution of the United States of America is dead. America has fallen, exactly as Benjamin Franklin predicted. It has ended in despotism.

The First Amendment is dead. The government now has the power to lock up dissenters of "free speech" without evidence or due process under the guise of "election interference" or "national defense", or other frivolous charges such as posting memes online. Political prisoners are currently incarcerated in the USA having committed no crime while those in power are career criminals themselves. You cannot speak the truth (or opinion) if that truth exposes the criminal lies of the establishment.

If you believe we have the right to the freedom of the press or freedom of religion, how do you explain Christians being forbidden from praying in schools while cross-dressing transgender Satanists freely prance around in underwear in front of helpless children? You can cling to your precious declaration all you want, but there is a reason *that* particular document is now housed in a taxpayer-funded history museum. Because it is history.

The Second Amendment is dead. This amendment states the people have the right to form a militia to overthrow a tyrannical government. Anyone who attempts to exercise the details of this "right" will be hunted down by the FBI, ATF, DHS, or any number of three-letter agencies under the facade of "domestic terrorism".

The Third Amendment is pointless because we *do* have a standing army, often occupied in its highest ranks by people who hate America. This standing army is "quartered" at the taxpayers' expense, with all expenses paid, for their entire lives if they wish, to stay employed in said army. All the while, the armed forces, whose mission it was to "defend the homeland" are off fighting wars in foreign lands for foreign interests at the behest of global elites.

The Fourth Amendment is dead. The unlawful searches and seizures taking place in America are countless. From local city officials entering your residence without your permission to "cite proper building code" if you so much as dare to build a small lean-to shed for your lawnmower, a garage for your tools, or a sitting room for you and your friends; to the use of force for "probable cause", to a former president being raided by law enforcement for doing what every other president before him has done… the illusions committed against the Fourth Amendment are endless. The right to personal property is over. People just haven't realized it yet.

But again, why does any of this matter knowing our kingdom is from another place? Nobody can take away what our Lord has given us!

The Fifth Amendment is also dead. In part, it states, "… nor be deprived of life, liberty, or property, without due process of law; nor shall private property be taken for public use, without just compensation." Not only do we the people *not* receive "just compensation" when the government takes our land, but we must pay the government in the form of taxation to *keep* the land we already own. Forget about the due process of law in the 5th, they will simply write a new law that nullifies the former. This happens all the time. Think about the Patriot Act or the NDAA's. Pleading the fifth means nothing if you never get your day in court.

The Sixth Amendment is dead. Anyone who claims we live in a society where "an impartial jury" and a speedy trial are a citizen's rights has blatantly ignored the common proceedings in our so-called justice system. There are neither speedy trials for the accused, nor an informed, unbiased judge or jury.

Skip to the Twelfth Amendment, fair Presidential elections… well, the jury is in on that one for sure and everyone

Christian Political Correctness

knows the emperor has no clothes. Need we be so redundant as to suggest the twelfth amendment is dead?

A person could pick through each amendment and every law in the USA, but what is the point when we know the document is no longer in standing practice? The republic is gone, Rome is burning, and there is no bringing it back no matter how forcefully the "Christian" pundits call us to arms. As Mr. Franklin mentioned some 200 years ago, their deistic efforts, "ended in despotism".

If you take anything away from this book, take this... despite the rise and fall of the once great American empire, Christ is still on his throne! Imagine that! No matter what the beast government does with *his* worldly empires, he is already defeated by the resurrection of Christ and Christ's new world order, coming soon to a city near you.

Eventually, Christ *will* return to earth when the time is fulfilled, and the Father deems it appropriate. No matter what governing authority was in power at that time, our King Jesus will set up his throne in Jerusalem for 1000 years, proving to every soul throughout history the proper way to manage a government. With love, truth, and *right*eousness, Christ will reign supreme as King of Heaven and Earth.

Thomas Jefferson was no stranger to religious squabbles either. During his Presidential campaign against John Adams in 1800, he was quoted as calling those opposed to his presidential campaign an "irritable tribe of priests". This man was never shy about lobbying to keep the name of Christ *out* of the Constitution, but in fact, he would argue for its insistence.

> Jefferson's campaign to end state support of religion fueled doubts about his personal religious beliefs. These doubts, which had swirled around him for years, emerged as a

> critical issue in the bitter presidential campaign of 1800. ... Like other Founding Fathers, Jefferson was considered a Deist, subscribing to the liberal religious strand of Deism that values reason over revelation and rejects traditional Christian doctrines, including the Virgin Birth, original sin and the resurrection of Jesus. While he rejected orthodoxy, Jefferson was nevertheless a religious man.[12]

Jefferson was a religious man... that's nice. Satan is also quite "religious". That does not mean we should form a government around *Satan's* personal preferences.

Did you know Thomas Jefferson edited the four gospels to suit his own personal beliefs, taking out many of the very important teachings of Christ? The entire Jefferson bible can be found online under the name, "The Life and Morals of Jesus of Nazareth"[13]. You can view for yourself every page; every snip and tuck, every cut and paste, and every rearrangement of the gospel as he saw fit. Link to this website in the endnotes.

> The Life and Morals of Jesus of Nazareth, created by Thomas Jefferson in 1820, is an 84-page assemblage of passages from the first four books of the New Testament. It was the work of Jefferson's own hands and a product of his extraordinary mind. It was a personal exercise in understanding Jesus's moral teachings. The resulting work represented a meeting of Enlightenment thought and Christian tradition as imagined by one of the great thinkers of the Revolutionary Era.
>
> Jefferson made no plans to publish this work; it was solely for his own reading and reflection. He knew that

his beliefs would offend some religious authorities and be used against him by his political rivals.

The book remained privately held throughout his life. Its existence was only known to a few of his closest circle of friends. The book remained in his family until his great-granddaughter sold the volume to the Smithsonian Institution in 1895.[13]

Why would one of the most predominant thinkers in American heritage hide from the public the fact that he secretly dissected the words of Christ throwing out the parts he didn't like?

It is theorized by free-thinking historians that Jefferson only included the four gospels, refusing to include the apostles' many letters to the church, because every single one of the apostles' letters confirmed Christ's teachings. How could you butcher the word of the son of God while simultaneously acknowledging his disciples? This may be in-and-of itself circumstantial evidence, but it is a valid question concerning the mounds of additional evidence at hand.

If it walks like a duck and talks like a duck, does that make it a Christian? No, that makes it a duck.

James Madison too was well equipped in the art of turning a phrase. "Resistance to tyranny is service to God", he once said.

"Our Constitution represents the work of the finger of Almighty God."

Hmm... bold statement. They believed their ink pens were the "finger of Almighty God". However, much like the rest of his deist brethren, they were never too keen on calling their god out by name. As a result of this obvious divestiture from Christ's teachings, the Christians among them would frequently protest.

> Although Madison was raised Episcopalian and attended St. John's Episcopal Church while he served as President of the United States, there is not much evidence leading to his personal religious beliefs. In fact, scholars tend to disagree about Madison's religion based on their own religious beliefs. For example, William C. Rives was Madison's nineteenth-century biographer and was also a pillar of the church in Virginia. He asserted that on Christianity's "doctrinal points" Madison was a model of "orthodoxy and penetration." Madison's twentieth-century biographer Irving Brant had no affiliation with the church and bluntly pronounced Madison a deist.[14]

They were, after all, politicians with a need to make their constituents happy. If their constituents were Christians, playing the part of a Christian was mandatory. *Playing the part* is just good business.

As noted previously, among the founding fathers were non-Christian deists, Christian deists, and orthodox Christians. Washington, Franklin, Jefferson, and the likes of their fellows had all ascribed to strict deism. John Adams however was one such *Christian* deist with quite the track record of interesting views of his own.

Adams once said, "Power always thinks... it is doing God's service when it is violating all his laws."

He could not have been more accurate. From the very beginning, they had already violated the governing laws of Christ to make way for their own endeavors.

The painful irony weaved into so much of this thread is listening to the founders in their own words. Their government had become a menace in foresight, and they all knew this was the case. Even in America's infancy, they made statements, confirmed in their own minds, how they had created a beast that could now no longer be controlled.

John Adams is one such man who noted these conclusions on multiple occasions.

> "There is nothing I dread so much as the division of the republic into two great parties, each arranged under its leader, and concerting measures in opposition to each other. This, in my humble apprehension, is to be dreaded as the greatest political evil under our constitution.
>
> "Democracy will soon degenerate into an anarchy, such an anarchy that *every man will do what is right in his own eyes* and no man's life or property or reputation or liberty will be secure, and every one of these will soon mold itself into a system of subordination of all the moral virtues and intellectual abilities, all the powers of wealth, beauty, wit and science, to the wanton pleasures, the capricious will, and the execrable cruelty of one or a very few.
>
> "Remember, democracy never lasts long. It soon wastes, exhausts, and murders itself. There never was a democracy yet that did not commit suicide."

The founders could seldom agree on much of anything. They were hopelessly divided as a result of not being founded on the solid rock of Christ's gospel. Their efforts were in vain, as would be any democratic republic claiming "God and Country" without naming the One True God and his only begotten son.

John Adams knew this to be true when he said, "But a Constitution of Government once changed from Freedom, can never be restored. Liberty, once lost, is lost forever."

As a legislator, Mr. Adams is right. As a Christian deist, he failed to mention that the only true liberty is found in Christ our savior which is *never* lost to those who adhere to his *right*eousness. The word of God will stand forever! (Matthew 24:35)

> "The Declaration of Independence laid the cornerstone of human government upon *the first precepts of Christianity*."

...said the person looking to save face with his constituents. Statements such as these are either an egregious lie, a political maneuver, or pure ignorance of the gospel message given by Christ. Their republic was not founded upon the "first precepts of Christianity", as has been noted continuously throughout this book. To suggest the founders' intentions were based on the teachings of Jesus Christ is intentionally deceptive. The above statement contradicts several of Adams' earlier statements, as well as the word-for-word core values of Christ's teachings.

Once again, we must state the obvious. If I kill a man in the name of Christ, it does not mean I am doing Christ's work, or that Christ instructed me to kill. If John Adams were still with us today, we could ask him this question, "what exactly are the first precepts of Christianity and how exactly were they implemented during the American Revolution?" To which he would likely be unable to give an honest answer based on the facts surrounding his immediate form of government.

Mr. Benjamin Rush, a known orthodox Christian, doctor, and psychiatrist, emphatically disagreed with the majority.

Christian Political Correctness

He among others are names the American Christian public has never heard nor known existed.

Should we beat this dead horse to death? Should we continue through every single letter, and every single quote of the American founding fathers?

An unbiased person could, if they desired, systematically navigate the countless statements presented by reading the founding father's letters in full[15]. A rendering of such in this book would be much too cumbersome for the reader. For this cause, a note is provided at the end of this book[15]. The reader can navigate the historical record themselves.

~

> "You know my heart wishes for peace upon terms of security and justice to America. But war, anything, is preferable to a surrender of our rights." ~ Thomas Stone

It is important to search the historical record. Finding direct quotes from the people who lived in that day while analyzing their life choices is a better resource than postulating over exactly how tyrannical their oppressors were based on a rewritten history.

> Stone had a large house, thousands of acres of land, and a young family, along with as many as 30 enslaved African Americans who performed the labor that supplied Stone's wealth. Frequent travel, *financial worries,* and concerns for his wife's health took a toll on Stone. He died at age 44 and barely lived to see an independent America.[16] (emphasis mine)

Philip Joel Walls

What could be the cause of Thomas Stone's "financial worries"? What led Mr. Stone to consider war as a better option than the peace he so desired?

We know for certain the "unfair banking practices" poised from England had all the colonial businessmen and politicians up in arms. They did not want the king of England regulating a currency they themselves were attempting to regulate. And now we hear affluent politicians state, "But war, anything, is preferable to a surrender of our rights."

To be clear, the "rights" he alluded to in this statement was the right to own land. After the French and Indian wars, and as the "moving west" continued, the right to own land was extremely important to damn near everybody on both sides of the war.

Something at that specific time in Stone's life was causing him to have "financial worries."

Why would a rich man have financial worries? Perhaps because his money was being devalued due to the overprinting of colonial currencies, and the King of England was tired of the colonies rebelling against his financial orders?

If Mr. Stone had done as Christ practiced and the apostles commanded, "slaves obey your masters", Who knows what would have happened? He *may* have eventually lost his fortunes due to the overprinting of colonial currency, and the subsequent Currency Acts from England. Unfortunately for Mr. Stone, that was too much for him to bear. War, as he said, was the only solution to his financial worries.

Ask yourself, how are these actions the result of following Christ's teachings? Was this nation truly founded on the "first precepts of Christianity"?

It must have been a great burden living a double life in this manner. On one hand, Stone kept a tribe of slaves as a labor force to benefit from their labor. On the other hand, he and his buddies whined and complained about how the king of England was not treating them fairly. Talk about the pot calling the kettle black.

Do you think these men ever sought counsel in their slaves asking, *"Come here, slave, I must ask you a question. I am having a difficult time with **my** master. I am indebted to the land I own and now the crown is asking for more than I can repay. What shall I do? I ask you, slave, what do you do when your master treats you unfavorably"*? to which the slave replies, *"master, I am your slave. I do as I am told, else, I am punished, sir."*

The above is hyperbole, but not altogether as disingenuous as complaining about your evil "tyrant" king when you yourself are a slave master reaping all the benefits from your slaves. How has this double-standard hypocrisy in America's "Christian heritage" gone unnoticed by modern Christians?

My "heart wishes for peace", says Mr. Stone. But my debts are piling up and I have no option left but to join forces with those who would choose war as the only option to absolve my debts to the King.

The "unfair banking practices" of the king of England are sure to have upset Mr. Stone (and all his friends in the continental congress) to the point where even though he wanted peace, he more so desired a "more perfect union" apart from those who owned his debt. When you have so much to lose… it is much more preferable to fight as a "patriot" in absolution to your debt, than it is to admit your sins and accept consequences for your actions.

~

There is a difference between the honest God-fearing Christians who would rather have stayed under the direction of the king of England (of whom there were many), than the abhorrent deists who chose to slaughter their Christian brethren for the sake of their own "liberty". That is a fact you will seldom hear from the Christian procurators of our day.

Yes, there were Christians in government at that time, but they too were being systematically dismantled by the devout deists and their powerful unspoken influence.

Benjamin Rush, a representative from Pennsylvania, had a great deal to say about these deists.

> We profess to be Republicans, and yet *we neglect* the only means of establishing and perpetuating our republican forms of government; that is, *the universal education of our youth in the principles of Christianity* by means of the Bible; for this divine book, above all others, favors that equality among mankind, that respect for just laws, and all those sober and frugal virtues which constitute the soul of republicanism. (emphasis mine)

Why would Mr. Rush make this statement? This is a direct contradiction to Adam's earlier statement about how the Constitution was founded on "the first precepts of Christianity". According to Rush, a Christian physician, the Continental Congress had been explicitly denying the precepts of Christianity. Why would Rush so adamantly suggest "we neglect" to teach Biblical Christianity to our children? Is that not an odd thing to say coming from a man who rubbed elbows with the likes of Thomas Jefferson, Benjamin Franklin, and John Adams while residing over Pennsylvania politics?

If Mr. Rush and his fellows were to have their way, this country *could* have more accurately been founded on Christian principles. Yet, how many times do you recall the name Benjamin Rush being cited in your high school history class?

> "Let the children...be carefully instructed in the principles and obligations of the Christian religion. This is the most essential part of education."

Perhaps this is why John Adams admitted after Rush's death...

> "Dr Rush was a greater and better Man than Dr Franklin: Yet Rush was always persecuted and Franklin always adored. ... Rush has done infinitely more good to America than Franklin. Both had deserved a high Rank among Benefactors to their Country and Mankind; but Rush by far the highest."

Many names were excluded from this chapter on our founding fathers. Not because I desire to hide facts or disillusion the reader, but because it would take too long to cite them all. Another series of books would be required to entertain the entirety. The above was assembled for the sake of clarity and insight. At least, it was meant to spark a flame of conscience.

I will now leave the reader with this final thought.

What good are we as modern American Christians if we fail to point out the obvious falsehoods in American history? In all our toils, death, blood, and warfare to preserve "a more perfect union", are we truly assembling as the hands and feet of Christ? Or are we in fact perverting Christ's name for the sake of our own comfortable religion, and Christian Political Correctness?

CHAPTER 5

A True Christian Nation

"For unto us a child is born, unto us a son is given: and *the government shall be upon his shoulder*: and his name shall be called Wonderful, Counseller, The mighty God, The everlasting Father, The Prince of Peace." (Isaiah 9:6)

In my best Rod Serling voice: *Imagine if you will, a people so exclusively devoted to the teachings of Christ, they no longer care who governs the land. They obey Jesus when he says, "love your enemies", and "thy kingdom come, thy will be done on earth, as it is in heaven".*

Enter a church so unique there is neither brick nor mortar, steeple nor stained glass, but only a heart seeking the lord in all walks of life.

Unknown by future inhabitants of this land, such a church would have been persecuted for refusing to go to war with their king. A king who defended their right to practice religion as they saw fit.

Consider now, it was none other than their patriotic Christian neighbors persecuting this church in the name of "God and Country".

Herein lies a land of such degradation and abuse of the gospel that it could only be founded by men living… in the Twilight Zone.

Alright, cut! Rod, what the h*** is *this*? When I agreed to produce this show, you told me we were creating science fiction, mystery, and fantasy. This will never appeal to our audience. Try using another line, try something different. Okay, ready, and… action.

…Come with me, if you will, into a land of such degradation that it could only be established in… a deistic republic.

Cut! Excellent, that's a wrap.

~

A true Christian nation would look nothing like a constitutional republic or a Western democracy. It would resemble a global community supernaturally woven together by the fabric of Christ's teachings despite whichever beast entity was governing their local society. It would not matter what form of government occupied the land, but only that the love of God and the gospel of Jesus Christ were governing the hearts of its citizens. There would be no need for manmade documents or redundant constitutional amendments justifying what is "right" or wrong because everyone would already know the true definition of *right*eousness. There would be no praise for "checks and balances" within a three-tiered system of executive, legislative, and judicial branches of government. The mob rules mentality of "voting for change" would be irrelevant. The *right*eousness of God is eternal and unchangeable. We cannot vote our way into the kingdom of heaven nor legislate the resurrection of our souls from hell. The truth of God exists whether we vote for it or not.

In a true Christian nation, there would be no national identity but only an exclusive realization of the universal authority of our King Jehoshua (Jesus). No matter what governmental structures regulate the laws of the land (China, Russia, USA, Saudi Arabia, Israel; all irrelevant), Christians would simply follow the laws of Christ; for better, or for worse.

We are commanded by our King Jehoshua to obey our earthly masters (to the extent it does not conflict with righteousness) and love our enemies. The *people* would in turn live in accordance with the teachings of the King of *Righteousness* given to us by Jesus Christ (High Priest over the order of Melchizedek; Genesis 14; Psalm 110; Hebrews 5, 6, 7; more on this later).

If the law of the land conflicts with true worship (such as bowing down to idols or being put to death; Daniel 3:4-6), we would need to faithfully accept the consequences of remaining true to God. But never are we commanded to form an army of "Christians" to kill our oppressors.

It truly is this simple. We don't need a government of oversight such as the Beast United Nations, a failed constitutional republic such as the American Foundation, nor a Christian Nationalist dictatorship such as that proposed by the extremists in modern "Christianity". *We the people* need *faith* and *perseverance* which is required by our submission to the will of God. It is God Himself who will repay vengeance to those who have persecuted and killed His servants.

We need a government of God reigning within our hearts, not a Christian dictatorship at the tips of our fingers.

The spirit of the Satanic beast system of government has penetrated every type of society to ever exist. Including, but not limited to, the origins of the American Constitutional Republic.

Jesus did not teach his disciples to spend their time and efforts seeking the establishment of a "more perfect union" here on earth. He taught them to repent; to call upon the name of the Father in all circumstances and in all prayer, to do the will of the Father.

> Our Father which art in heaven, Hallowed be thy name. Thy kingdom come. Thy will be done in earth, as it is in heaven. (Matthew 6:9-10)

> I can of mine own self do nothing: as I hear, I judge: and my judgment is just; because I seek not mine own will, but the will of the Father which hath sent me. (John 5:30)

There may be no greater quote from Jesus regarding his role as the High Priest over the order of Melchizedek than John 5:30. Jesus was fulfilling the will of the Father in heaven. That is our role as subjects under God's government. To do the will of God. This instruction in *right*eousness was the sole purpose of all priests under this order. Jesus said not even *he* was able to change the circumstances of the Father's will. Who do we think we are to claim *we* are going to *create* "a more perfect union" based on *our* own understanding?

This phrase, "Hallowed by thy name", is beautiful and poetic in the old English dialect, but it is a bit lacking in its broader meaning. It could more accurately be translated as "Your name should be Hallowed (G37; *hagiazó*; to make holy, consecrate, sanctify). It is not simply us acknowledging that God's name is already Holy, which is true, but that we are actively engaging in hallowing His name. "Hallowed by thy name" is the same as stating, "your name shall be hallowed".

Christian Political Correctness

Hallowing His name would be the exact opposite of taking the name of God in vain. If we are using the name of God in vain (using His name for vain purposes or agendas), we are not "hallowing" our God's name. And if we are hallowing His name, it is us actively praising and proclaiming His *right*eousness on earth. *"Let your name be hallowed in all the earth, let your kingdom come to earth, let your will be done on earth; as it is in heaven."*

But what has mankind done? We have used the name of "God" for so many atrocities that His Kingdom is nowhere to be found outside the hearts of those who love and obey the *King* of *Right*eousness.

Jesus' statement in Matthew 6 regarding proper prayer has nothing to do with us ***asking*** for a "hallowing" of God's name, but everything to do with us ***actively*** "hallowing" His name and allowing the Father's will be done in our lives. The will of the Father, through the teachings of His only begotten son, Jesus Christ.

Jesus did not come on his own accord, but because his Father sent him. Listening to Jesus is listening to God. Doing the will of Jesus is doing the will of God because Jesus is God's personal representative (his only begotten son) on planet Earth. We do not need an earthly government. We need to obey Jesus and do the will of his Father; God.

Furthermore, Jesus told us not to call anyone "father" because there is only one father, the Father in heaven.

> And call no man your father upon the earth: for one is your Father, which is in heaven. 10Neither be ye called masters: for one is your Master, even Christ. 11But he that is greatest among you shall be your servant. 12And whosoever shall exalt himself shall be abased; and he that shall humble himself shall be exalted. (Matthew 23:9-12)

Understand, we can seek the will of our Father in heaven, or we can seek the will of the American founding "fathers". But we cannot do both.

At the end of this line of truth, there is only one conclusion. When all is said and done, the anti-Christ deists *did* ultimately succeed in forming their republic while the outspoken Christians such as Benjamin Rush and others lost the debate without measure. Christ was pushed out of the American Constitution while "Natures God" was inserted. Their deistic ideals were officially institutionalized as the law of the land while the laws of Christ and his heavenly Father were excluded. No matter how the Christian Nationalists tried to wrap the American flag around *the Holy Bible* or hang the Ten Commandments in national buildings, their republic was little more than a house of cards built on quicksand.

If the United States of America were a boat, the ship has long since sailed and sunk to the depths of the sea.

Ask yourself, are God and Jesus Christ the head of our Constitutional Republic, or is something else running the show? Are God's laws being followed in the USA, or are the doctrines of men more prevalent? Are the virtues of Christ a beacon shining brightly from that "city on the hill", or have we Christians been participating in the greatest religious hoax of the common era?

A simple reading of the Christian New Testament gospel as it was written will provide definitive answers to these questions.

~

What benefit does politically correct Christianity supply to America? What gain does Christian political correctness give to the Western world as a whole? Have we ever stopped to consider the repercussions of institutionalizing false Christian doctrine and false history from the governmental level? For instance, what does our strong affiliation with Zionist Israel do to the nature of true Christianity among our Muslim brothers and sisters throughout the world? Does this bias against Muslims help us or hinder us as a "Christian nation"?

It is well known that both Jews and Muslims reject Jesus as the Messiah. It is much less known that Islam considers Jesus a great prophet while the Talmudic Jews claim Jesus is boiling in human excrement in the pits of hell. Yet, we consider the modern nation of Israel a Christian ally, and the universal nation of Islam an enemy. Why? Who is preaching a more anti-Christ doctrine; the Muslims who believe Christ was a great prophet, or our supposedly Jewish friends in Israel who believe Jesus is currently burning in hell?

The nation of Israel rejects Jesus as the Messiah based on many factors. Not least of which, they believe *their* messiah will be a conquering force here on planet Earth. Since Jesus was, in their eyes, killed by the Romans, he (Jesus) did not fulfill the prophecies of a conquering messiah. This is what "Israel" is currently waiting for. A messiah to conquer all the nations of the earth here in this timeline.

The nation of Islam also rejects Jesus as the Messiah but for significantly different reasons. One of the lesser reasons, yet not dismissible, is that our Western European and American politicians often portray themselves as "Christians". Due to this, the nation of Islam sees Christians as not only hypocrites but as direct contributors to the Satanic forces on earth.

These Western politicians: these wolves in sheep's clothing, these liars, these demons "playing the part" have for many decades been dropping bombs on Muslim countries as a result of their foreign interests and political ties to

"Israel". This is why the Mullahs in Tehran have referred to "Christian" America and "Jewish" Israel as the "great Satan" and the "little Satan", respectively.

Frankly, even though they (Tehran) are not *righteous* themselves, they are not wrong about America. Our false Christianity and support of Zionist "Israel" at the governmental level is one reason why certain members of Islam are so angry with the United States. Having false Christians representing a nation of a predominantly Christian population is very bad for relations with non-Christian nations.

False Christianity in American government is not now, nor ever was, nor ever will be an accurate representation of true Christianity around the world. It only serves to prove beyond the shadow of a doubt how the wolves dressed in sheep's clothing, those who run the US government, are false Christians. There is a monumental difference between God-fearing Christians and politically correct Christians.

> Take heed that no man deceive you. 5For many shall come in my name, saying, I am Christ; and shall deceive many. (Matthew 24:4-5)

> For such are false apostles, deceitful workers, transforming themselves into the apostles of Christ. (2 Corinthians 11:13)

> I know thy works, and tribulation, and poverty, (but thou art rich) and I know the blasphemy of them which say they are Jews, and are not, but are the synagogue of Satan. (Revelation 2:9)

Christian Political Correctness

If Jim Jones called himself a Pentecostal Christian (which he did) does that make him a Christian? No, it makes him a delusional psychopath.

If wolves like Peter Popoff claim to be apostles of Christ curing poverty and sickness worldwide via *your* financial donations, does that make them Christians? No, dear reader. It makes them false teachers and false healers.

If George H.W. Bush called himself a Christian for attending St. Martin's Episcopal Church in Houston, Texas for nearly fifty years, does that make him a Christian? No, it makes him; a member of Skull and Bones secret backdoor club, Ambassador to the UN under President Nixon, Director of the CIA under President Ford, President of the United States during the first Gulf War, and likely an instrumental character in the assassination of JFK as explained thoroughly in the documentary "Dark Legacy". He was *not* a Christian.

Playing the part of a Christian is very important to businessmen and politicians, the same way it was important to the American founding "fathers". None of these men were followers of Christ, not by any means. So, what happens when *they* are the face of our "Christian Nation" around the globe?

Are you starting to understand how this works?

Many in the Muslim world (particularly the Mullahs in Tehran, but there are other sects) still view the United States and Israel as the hands and feet of Satan. Why? Because people like George Bush were voted into office through the government of our "Christian nation". Because **we the people** vote these wolves into office. Our leaders then turn about-face tramping off into foreign lands to start wars at the behest of their handlers. No wonder so many Muslims hate America. Why wouldn't they?

Now... consider this *very* carefully.

If "Christians" throughout history had been acting in accordance with Christ's commands, our history books would read much differently. There would have been no crusades from England to conquer the Holy Land. No wars among varying sects of Catholics vs. Anglicans. The American founding "fathers" would have never butchered the non-resistant Christians for the sake of their own "liberty". Additionally, for the sake of this debate, there would have been no wars with Muslim countries throughout the Middle East during our modern era. And therefore, the nation of Islam would not hate America the way it does.

What exactly is the motivation of Western governments? If we are now, or ever were a Christian nation, and if our American Republic truly was adhering to the will of God, the Muslim nations across the globe would have no reason to hate us, because we would not be invading their sovereign territories demanding western democracy (or the monarchy of England; or by Papal decree; or Zionist Israel), killing anyone who gets in the way of the agenda.

If we remain loyal to Politically Correct Christianity (including Evangelical Westerners, Anglicanism, Catholicism, and/or Zionism), attempting to conquer the world in the name of peace, we will be denying the will of God and forfeiting our souls to hellfire.

The death of a Muslim believer at the hands of a Christian sword is the work of Satan. You can quote me on that, too.

According to the bible, we (Muslims and Christians) *could* collectively, based on *the Holy Bible*, agree that our Almighty God is on His throne. That Jesus is the son of God (not God Himself) who came to earth as a teacher of *right*eousness and as a means to an end to rid humanity of the sin problem once and for all. Because he *is* the begotten son of God, and because he lived a sinless life in truth and *right*eousness, he was worthy and willing to sacrifice his own life as an atonement for the sins of mankind.

Most Christians don't know this, but the Qur'an states Jesus was greater than all other prophets. Meanwhile, the modern "Jews" believe Jesus is burning in hell for his blasphemy.

If America were acting like the hands and feet of Christ, and not those of idolatrous and blasphemous works, the Islamic world would be much more inclined to listen when we say Jesus is the son of God. His life was not taken from him, but he willingly offered his life as a sacrifice.

> I am the good shepherd, and know my sheep, and am known of mine. 15As the Father knoweth me, even so know I the Father: and I lay down my life for the sheep. 16*And other sheep I have, which are not of this fold*: them also I must bring, *and they shall hear my voice*; and there shall be one fold, and one shepherd. 17Therefore doth my Father love me, because I lay down my life, that I might take it again. 18No man taketh it from me, but I lay it down of myself. I have power to lay it down, and I have power to take it again. This commandment have I received of my Father. (John 10:14-18)

> The Lord is not slack concerning his promise, as some men count slackness; but is longsuffering to us-ward, not willing that any should perish, *but that **all** should come to repentance*. (2 Peter 3:9)

Who are we to claim Muslims are excluded from the love of God through Christ Jesus? Muslims already know Jesus was a great prophet. Jesus "Isa" is mentioned more than ninety times in fifteen different Surahs.[17] The Qur'an considers Jesus' superior to all other prophets; was born of a virgin, performed miracles, and lived a sinless life. However, they do not believe in the resurrection and emphatically deny that Jesus *is* God. Armed with this knowledge in the Qur'an, combined with the work of Dr. Thomas Allen Rexroth[18] citing the fundamental nature of Jesus Christ, the work done by Josh McDowell[viii] citing the historical evidence for the resurrection of Jesus, as well as the earth-shattering information found in Chick Publications "The Prophet"[19], a great number of Muslims could easily be persuaded to faithfully accept Isa (Jesus) as their Messiah. They could come to know in their hearts how ***true*** Christians are not the enemy.

Still, the problem remains... the *false* Christians are out there running the gambit. They are still in charge of our western government.

Earlier, I posed the question, "what benefit does politically correct Christianity supply to America? What gain does Christian political correctness give to the Western world as a whole?" The answer is, death and un-*right*eousness. This is the benefit Christian Political Correctness brings to America and the Western world. Death and un*right*eousness.

May God have mercy on us all for what we have done. If it were not for our bought and paid-for elected officials, these wolves in sheep's clothing 'playing the part', we would have a much more peaceful world. The chaos in the world today is a great deal in part the result of an anti-Christ nation with "Christian" Nationalists (including Zionist "Israel") using the name of "God" and Christ to accomplish an agenda. All the while, they have no intention whatsoever to seek the will of God and *His righteousness*. They have corrupted their ways and their hearts are *far* from the will of God.

If the United States of America were in fact built on the "first precepts of Christianity" as opposed to blindly following our deistic founding "fathers", the chaos across this planet would not be what it is today.

~

Many people will point to *the Holy Bible* to suggest democracy is a sound Christian teaching. Acts 6 is one such familiar passage.

> Now at this time, as the disciples were increasing in number, a complaint developed on the part of the Hellenistic Jews against the native Hebrews, because their widows were being overlooked in the daily serving of food. 2So the twelve summoned the congregation of the disciples and said, "It is not desirable for us to neglect the word of God in order to serve tables. Instead, brothers and sisters, *select from among you seven men of good reputation*, full of the Spirit and of wisdom, whom we may put in charge of this task. 4But we will devote ourselves to prayer and to the ministry of the word." 5The announcement found approval with the whole congregation; *and they chose* Stephen, a man full of faith and of the Holy Spirit, and Philip, Prochorus, Nicanor, Timon, Parmenas, and Nicolas, a proselyte from Antioch. 6And they brought these men before the apostles; and after praying, they laid their hands on them. (Acts 6:3-6; NAS)

Ah ha! Did you hear what they said? Democracy is biblical! They were voting for leaders! Yes, the apostles asked the congregation to choose seven men from among them to be placed in charge of the distribution of food. They did this because the number of disciples was increasing and the apostles no longer had time to travel from house to house distributing food, which is one of the jobs of the church. Feeding the poor and needy in the community. So, the apostles asked the disciples to handle this task themselves. This way, the apostles could continue focusing on evangelism. What the Apostles did **not** say was, "*Rome is persecuting our people. I want you to form an army to fight against anyone who opposes our financial system of distributing food for free. We will build a new democratic republic of our own to see this through to fruition.*" That much *should* be obvious. But it is not. People want to oversee themselves (democracy) and make their own decisions. They do not want God telling them what to do (hence Christian deism). By using the name of God and Christ, they are playing Christian politics by personally stamping God's seal of approval on *their* democratic republic.

Christian deism (the cornerstone of Christian Nationalism) and a democratic republic is a perfect recipe to not only have carte blanche to govern yourself, but to openly dismiss the word of God while simultaneously calling yourself a "Christian".

~

Did you know the only form of government ever ordained by God was a monarchy? (1 Samuel 8) Not a democracy, nor a republic, but a monarchy. And the only reason God allowed this transition from Judges to Kings to take place was due to the people's hardness of heart. But before the era of the kings became the established government in Israel, the people of Israel were judged by the high priest under the order of Melchizedek. In other words, the people of Israel were *governed* by Judges, Priests, and Prophets. That was the only form of government necessary for God's people. They would either prosper in the land as a result of listening to the judges, or they would kindle the wrath of God by ignoring them.

> Nevertheless *the LORD raised up judges,* which delivered them out of the hand of those that spoiled them. 17And yet they would not hearken unto their judges, but they went whoring after other gods, and bowed themselves unto them: they turned quickly out of the way which their fathers walked in, obeying the commandments of the LORD; but they did not so. 18And when the LORD raised them up judges, then *the LORD was with the judge,* and delivered them out of the hand of their enemies all the days of the judge: for it repented the LORD because of their groanings by reason of them that oppressed them and vexed them. 19And it came to pass, when the judge was dead, that they returned, and corrupted themselves more than their fathers, in following other gods to serve them, and to bow down unto them; *they ceased not from their own doings, nor from their stubborn way.* (Judges 2:16-19)

Read the first few chapters of Judges. Notice how when the people of Israel had rejected the LORD God by dismissing the testimony of their judges (or when their judges had died and left them to their own devices) they would "corrupt themselves more than their fathers". However, when they had a worthy judge among them, they would prosper. Again, this was the only form of government required in the eyes of God. If the nation were to listen to God's judgement, they would be fine. It truly is that simple.

As the years passed, the people of Israel would more and more reject the God Most High; their King of *Right*eousness. They possessed no further desire to be told what to do by their judges and priests. They wanted an *earthly* king. Someone they could see and touch. A *man* with whom they could plead their case. They wanted an approachable subject to the likes of the pagan nations they had come to love and admire. Their stiffness of heart was noticed by the LORD God. At that point, God decided He would let them 'have their head' for a while by allowing them to govern themselves. At the time of this transition, it was the prophet Samuel who was the judge and priest *filling in* under the order of Melchizedek.

> Then all the elders of Israel gathered together and came to Samuel at Ramah; 5and they said to him, "Behold, you have grown old, and your sons do not walk in your ways. Now appoint us a king to judge us like all the nations." 6But the matter was displeasing in the sight of Samuel when they said, "Give us a king to judge us." And Samuel prayed to the LORD. 7And the LORD said to Samuel, "Listen to the voice of the people regarding all that they say to you, because they have not rejected you, but they have rejected Me from being King over them. 8Like all the deeds which they have done since the day that I brought them up from Egypt even to this day—in that they have abandoned Me and served other gods—so they are doing to you as well. 9Now then, listen to their voice; however, you shall warn them strongly and tell them of the practice of the king who will reign over them." (1 Samuel 8:4-9; NAS)

In verses 5 and 6, the people informed Samuel that because his children had corrupted their ways, there would be no priest, judge, or prophet after he died (just like it said back in Judges 2). Knowing this, the stiff hearts of these men devised a plan to persuade Samuel to give them a king instead of a judge. "Give us a king to judge us." (v.6)

Notice the prophetic warning given by Samuel (from God) about what will happen to Israel when they seek their own government (a king) instead of relying on God's judgement (Melchizedek; King of *right*eousness) for His protection. God told Samuel to give the people of Israel exactly what they had been asking for. The absence of His presence.

God prophesied that because of their stiff hearts, they would no longer be a free people (1 Samuel 8:10-18). He told them their children would now be slaves to the king's wars (v.11). They would be slaves to labor in the field for the king's harvest, and slaves to the commander of arms (v.12). The king would take from their woman all whom he desired to work in his kitchens (v.13). The king would now take a tenth of everything produced in their fields for his own personal use (v.14-15). Above all, God told them the king would now take male and female servants of anyone he chose as well as the best of all livestock to be his own personal workforce. God told Samuel to warn the people of Israel how by following their own plans they would become slaves to their earthly king.

> "...and you yourselves will become his servants. 18Then you will cry out on that day because of your king whom you have chosen for yourselves, *but the LORD will not answer you on that day.*" 19Yet the people refused to listen to the voice of Samuel, and they said, *"No, but there shall be a king over us, 20so that we also may be like all the nations, and our king may judge us and go out before us and fight our battles."* 21Now after Samuel had heard all the words of the people, he repeated them in the LORD'S hearing. 22And the LORD said to Samuel, "Listen to their voice and appoint a king for them." (1 Samuel 8:17-22; NAS)

How much better are we Americans for desiring a "more perfect union" of our own design? What was the outcome of our founding "fathers" choosing their own methods of government as opposed to relying on God for His? At this point, the answer should be staring you in the face. We have become slaves in this land because we follow man's rules instead of God's rules. It should be noted how the Amish are the closest thing to a free people in all the Western world, but even they are subject to *the Beast* to a certain extent.

As Mr. Sasquatch once told me, "It goes without saying" that neither a republic "of the people" nor a democratic society are in any way characteristics of God and *His Right*eousness. The American founders were following the commandments of men rather than the commandments of God's only begotten son, Jesus Christ, the High Priest under the order of Melchizedek. ***This*** is God's supernatural government on planet Earth. This is the only government we ever truly needed.

~

The Order of Melchizedek

Melchizedek; [malki-tsedeq; from H4428-*melek*, meaning "king", and H6664-*tsedeq*, meaning "righteous", i.e. "king of righteousness" or "my king is right"]; Genesis 14; Psalm 110; Hebrews 5, 6, 7).

Before Saul or David ever graced the pages of scripture as the first kings of Israel, God's people were instructed by the standing judges, priests, or prophets. This was a very simple and effective form of government acknowledging God is in charge. Nothing else was required.

Christian Political Correctness

It can be shown that God's messengers in the flesh came from all walks of life and were referred to by different names and titles. Judges, priests, prophets, apostles, disciples, etc. In *every* case, they were following the same orders. God's orders. No matter which title was applied to them, they were faithfully serving the *King* of *Right*eousness, exclusively.

"Governments" as we know them today are never necessary. These modern manmade institutions are the result of mankind believing we can somehow sufficiently judge ourselves. As has been proven time and time again throughout all recorded history, nothing could be farther from the truth. Mankind is *not* capable of governing himself appropriately. This is no doubt why God has always, throughout every point in history, had *someone* proclaiming His name ("Hallowed by thy name") on the face of the earth. From the beginning of time, until the day Christ (Jesus) graced us with his presence, it has always been this way. The order of Melchizedek has always stood and will always stand as the authoritative word regarding God's *Right*eous Government. This is *exactly* why Jesus is referred to as the High Priest of this order (Hebrew 5:5-10).

This understanding is first introduced in Genesis 14. It is this individual (the king of Salem: known to be an area in Palestine) who was in the position of the priesthood at that time, reporting directly to God – following God's orders and proclaiming God's righteousness to the people of the land. (It should be noted how some believe this figure "Melchizedek" is Jesus himself in a pre-incarnation flesh. That debate is currently irrelevant due to the nature of *this* discussion. The main point being, we should follow God's government, not man's government.)

> And Melchizedek king of Salem brought forth bread and wine: and *he was the priest of the most high God*. And he blessed him, and said, Blessed be Abram of the most high God, possessor of heaven and earth: 20And blessed be the most high God, which hath delivered thine enemies into thy hand. And he gave him tithes of all. (Genesis 14:18-20)

This "Melchizedek" only shows up two times in the entirety of the Old Testament. However, we *can* piece together the facts based on common sense biblical investigation and the scriptures available to us on this topic.

> The LORD hath sworn, and will not repent, Thou art a priest for ever after the order of Melchizedek. 5*The Lord at thy right hand* shall strike through kings in the day of his wrath. 6He shall judge among the heathen, he shall fill the places with the dead bodies; he shall wound the heads over many countries. (Psalm 110:4-6)

In this Psalm, David is clearly not referring to himself. The only *one* sitting at the right hand of God is our Lord Jesus Christ. David knew this. He not only knew Jehoshua was at God's right hand (in the prophetical sense), destined to be the Messiah, but that Jesus was appointed as High Priest over the order of Melchizedek. This very well may have been common knowledge to the devout men of antiquity. At some point, people likely stopped talking about it. They stopped seeking God's *right*eousness (they pursued other gods) and dismissed this "order" altogether. This could be one reason it is mentioned so seldom in other parts of the Old Testament, as well as being so misunderstood by our churches and governments today. Why would we talk about the *righ*teousness of God's government when we are so hell-bent on forming a "more perfect union" of our own design?

To fully illustrate this position, we need to understand why Jesus is called the High Priest of this order.

In Revelation 3:7 and Isaiah 22:22 Jesus is depicted as being the fulfillment of the house of David (the "Key of David") or rather, the fulfillment of the line of Kings. This is to say there will never be another king under the authority of God sitting on the throne of Israel. Jesus is the first and last king. The King of *Righ*teousness. From the Davidic covenant to the time of Christ. This lineage was not broken. There was always someone "filling in" until Jesus arrived. Jesus is now in possession of the "Key of David" as the final King of Israel. It is the same understanding as the order of Melchizedek. There was always someone acting in place of the High Priest or "filling-in" on behalf of the priest, but not the high priest themselves.

Even though the name "Mechizedek" is not mentioned, we find more evidence in Jeremiah 33:14-26.

> For thus saith the LORD; *David shall never want a man to sit upon the throne of the house of Israel;* 18*Neither shall the priests the Levites want a man before me* to offer burnt offerings, and to kindle meat offerings, and to do sacrifice continually. (Jeremiah 33:17-18)

Jesus was the end of all sacrifice offerings. He was a sacrifice offering, by the way, that would never have been necessary if the people had been adhering to the *righ*teousness of God as opposed to following the deceptions of the devil (Genesis 2-3). Jesus willingly gave up his life as an atonement for the sins of mankind.

Jesus was the end of the sacrifice offering in the same way he was the end of the line of the Kings of Israel; in the same way, he is the final priest under this order. Jesus was and is the final call to repentance. He now stands in his rightful place as not only the sacrificial lamb of God, the final High Priest, and the final King of Israel, but King of Heaven and Earth – forever.

If this book were a 4th of July fireworks show, you could say *this* is our grand finale. Jesus was the end to the successors standing in his place as High Priest over the order of Mechizedek. All things came to an end when Jesus' sacrifice was fulfilled on the cross. He was and is, and will forever be, 1) the sacrificial lamb of God who takes away the sins of the world, 2) the promised Messiah who fulfilled all God-breathed scripture, 3) High Priest over the order of Melchizedek, 4) King of heaven and earth, and 5) **Governor** over all creation.

> All the ends of the world shall remember and turn unto the LORD: and all the kindreds of the nations shall worship before thee. 28For the kingdom is the LORD'S: and *he is the **governor** among the nations*. (Psalm 22:28; emphasis mine throughout)

> For unto us a child is born, unto us a son is given: and *the **government** shall be upon his shoulder*: and his name shall be called Wonderful, Counsellor, The mighty God, The everlasting Father, The Prince of Peace. 7Of *the increase of his **government** and peace there shall be no end,* upon the throne of David, and upon his kingdom, to order it, and *to establish it with judgment and with justice from henceforth even for ever*. The zeal of the LORD of hosts will perform this. (Isaiah 9:6-7)

Christian Political Correctness

> And thou Bethlehem, in the land of Juda, art not the least among the princes of Juda: for *out of thee shall come a Governor*, that shall rule my people Israel. (Matthew 2:6)

This word "governor" (H4951; *misrah*; to rule, dominion | G4165; *poimainó*; to govern as a shepherd) is used in reference to Jesus' authority to rule in the kingdom of God i.e. God's Government in heaven and on earth. We do not need any other form of government! Especially not a constitutional republic created by deists who rejected Christ as our King of *Right*eousness.

> No one takes this honor upon himself; he must be called by God, just as Aaron was [*the Aaronic line of priests*]. 5So also Christ did not take upon Himself the glory of becoming a high priest, but He was called by the One who said to Him: "You are My Son; today I have become Your Father." 6And in another passage God says: "You are a priest forever in the order of Melchizedek." 7During the days of Jesus' earthly life, He offered up prayers and petitions with loud cries and tears to the One who could save Him from death, and He was heard because of His reverence. 8Although He was a Son, He learned obedience from what He suffered. 9And having been made perfect, He became the source of eternal salvation to all who obey Him 10and was designated by God as high priest in the order of Melchizedek. (Hebrews 5:4-10; BSB; emphasis mine)

Jesus is called our Governor, King, and High Priest because he is the final authority over this holy and *right*eous priesthood – the order of Melchizedek.

Jesus Christ is the only Government ever ordained by God, of which He is very well pleased. Dearly beloved of

God, Jesus Christ is the only government we need in modern society.

The governments of this world are damned because they have no relationship with the true and *right*eous judgement found only in Christ Jesus.

~

Before the time of King David, there was never an official government or king overseeing God's people. There were only priests and judges reporting directly to God. God Himself was their Government and He was the only government they needed. He *should* be the only government *we* require. By adhering to the teachings of the King of *Right*eousness (Melchizedek; "my king is right"; in the personage of Jehoshua the Christ) we are fulfilling our duties as God's chosen people. We should be a people whose hearts are *governed* by God, and not by man.

No biblical evidence exists to suggest a constitutional republic is a God-inspired principle. In fact, there may be no greater manmade teaching in all the world than to suggest we humans have the ability to govern ourselves. Take a good long objective look back through history and ask yourself, how sufficiently has self-government been working? What benefits have come from claiming *we* possess the wit and wisdom to govern our own actions?

There is an old saying, '*Insanity is doing the same thing over and over again and expecting different results.*' In this regard, the people of the world are completely insane in attempting to govern themselves. We have failed every attempt in every way. There is no disputing this fact. When a new system of government in a new nation shows up on the scene, it always

Christian Political Correctness

and in every case is either born of or leads to chaos; war, hunger, poverty, famines, and not least of all, God's wrath.

It is time to repent. We need to place our faith in God and His only begotten son, our righteous King Jehoshua, the lamb of God, our good Shephard and Governor, our personal savior, the promised Messiah.

A true Christian nation would not care who manages the earthly territories because God and His *righ*teous son oversee all creation, and the new creation soon to be unveiled.

Can the American founding fathers bring your soul back from the dead?

Can the Constitution of the United States of America take away your sins and forgive your iniquity?

No, my friend. Only Christ has the authority to accomplish this task. Accepting Jesus as the atonement for sin while seeking the kingdom of God and His *righ*teousness is the only path to forgiveness.

Why place your faith in a republic founded by men who denied Christ's authority on earth? Why place your faith in a government where the founders themselves claimed despotism was inevitable? Saving the republic is no more "patriotism" than it is insanity, worshiping the idols of false deistic gods.

This is all very difficult for people to accept having been brainwashed by modern "Christianity" for so many years, but this is in fact what Christ taught. A true Christian nation would be subject to their masters as slaves. We are taught to obey our masters, even when they are harsh and unfair. We are taught to love our enemies even when they hate us and revile us in Jesus' name.

Let us not lean on our own understanding. Let us lift up and proclaim His glorious name on all the earth. Let us pray that His will be done on earth according to His *righ*teous judgement no matter how difficult the trials become. Let us praise God for the gift of His son who by his mortal sacrifice has created an atonement for the sins of mankind. Praise be to God forever, and forever. Amen.

Endnotes

1 Gerry Burney, *2068 Video Series*, (Target Truth Ministries, 2023), https://targettruthministries.com/#end
2 Philip Walls, *The Christian Doctrine Paradox* (Genesis Publishing House, 2022), 177-178
3 https://www.youtube.com/watch?v=yEP39YSF2Vk
4 https://doctrineparadox.com/the-evil-god-of-love/
5 Andrew J. O'Shaughnessy, *The Meeting of Thomas Jefferson, John Adams, and George III* (University of Vergina, 2019), https://engagement.virginia.edu/learn/2019/07/11/the-meeting-of-thomas-jefferson-john-adams-and-george-iii
6 Kevan D. Keane, *Persecution of Christians During the American Revolution* (Liberty University, 2015), https://digitalcommons.liberty.edu/symp_grad/2015/A/5/; https://digitalcommons.liberty.edu/cgi/viewcontent.cgi?article=1020&context=symp_grad
7 Margaret E. Hirst and Jones, Rufus M., *The Quakers in Peace and War*, Kessinger Publishing, 2010, p. 50; quoted in Bender, Wilbur J., "*Pacifism among the Mennonites, Amish Mennonites and Schwenkfelders to 1783,*" The

    Mennonite Quarterly Review, 1927, p. 32-33. (further quote from reference [vi] herein)
8 Josh McDowell, The New Evidence that Demands a Verdict (Nashville: Thomas Nelson 1999)
9 Longley, Robert. "The Currency Act of 1764." ThoughtCo, Aug. 9, 2021, thoughtco.com/currency-act-of-1764-104858.
10 https://www.britannica.com/topic/The-Founding-Fathers-Deism-and-Christianity-1272214
11 https://www.reddit.com/r/AskAnAmerican/comments/pvvzt9/what_is_the_deal_with_george_washington_and_the/?rdt=59745
12 https://www.pbs.org/wgbh/pages/frontline/godinamerica/people/thomas-jefferson.html
13 https://americanhistory.si.edu/JeffersonBible/history/#1
14 https://people.smu.edu/religionandfoundingusa/james-madisons-memorial-and-remonstrance/james-madison/
15 https://www.founders.archives.gov/
16 https://www.nps.gov/people/thomas-stone.htm
17 https://www.namb.net/apologetics/resource/a-comprehensive-listing-of-references-to-jesus-isa-in-the-qur-an/
18 Dr. Tomas Allen Rexroth, *Stumbling Block* (Genesis Publishing House, 2024)
19 Alberto R. Rivera, The *Prophet* (Ontario, CA, Chick Publications Inc., 1988)

Printed in the USA
CPSIA information can be obtained
at www.ICGtesting.com
CBHW072129110724
11457CB00024B/979